MANAGEMENT

A Practical Guide to Enhancing Managerial Effectiveness

OTHER BOOKS BY D.B.N. MURTHY

Disaster Management
Environmental Awareness and Protection
Environmental Planning and Management
Consumer and Quality
Living for Others
Of Man and Management
Of Man and Mountains
Of Men and Places
Managing Human Resources
Managing Quality
The Uncommon Doctor

MANAGEMENT

A Practical Guide to Enhancing Managerial Effectiveness

D.B.N. MURTHY

DEEP & DEEP PUBLICATIONS PVT. LTD.
F-159, Rajouri Garden, New Delhi - 110 027

MANAGEMENT
A Practical Guide to Enhancing Managerial Effectiveness

ISBN 978-81-8450-189-6

Typeset by RAHUL COMPOSERS
358, Pocket-B, Phase-II, Sector-16B, Dwarka, New Delhi - 110 078

Printed in India at MAYUR ENTERPRISES
WZ Plot No. 3, Gujjar Market, Tihar Village, New Delhi - 110 018

Published by DEEP & DEEP PUBLICATIONS PVT. LTD.,
F-159, Rajouri Garden, New Delhi - 110 027 • Phone : 25435369, 25440916
E-mail : ddpbooks@yahoo.co.in • ddpubs@gmail.com
Showroom :
2/13, Ansari Road, Daryaganj, New Delhi - 110 002 • Telefax : 23245122

In memory of
my dear wife Vimala

Contents

Preface

When I first wrote the book on management titled *"Of Man and Management"* in 1994, winds of change were already blowing on the economic scene which directly and indirectly affected management practices. With the liberalization and globalization in full swing, we have now a situation of 'problem of plenty' as far as consumer goods and services are concerned rather than acute shortages and long waiting periods as encountered in the past. The consumers of today had never had it so good. Obviously, there has been a change in the way we do business and consequently adaptation of a few management tools and techniques. However, time-tested strategies are as much relevant now as in the past, for example being customer-friendly and customer-focus the *raison d'etre* for any business worth its name. There is less emphasis on Japanese techniques and success stories at present compared to the past. We are now looking at the strategies of the best-managed companies that serve as benchmark around the world. That only means the manager of today perforce has to unlearn a few and learn a few other management practices that are relevant now.

Management is both an art and science. Those who study management techniques *et. al.* at business schools/colleges have an edge over others who have come up from the ranks and who depend upon more on their self-study, work experience and common sense, which is sometimes is an uncommon sense too! As we go along in our career we pick up techniques that we consider important. However, what is needed is the right choice of a tool at the right time for the right place. One might have acquired a complete set of 'tools' but they have to be used with caution and that too judiciously. There is no substitute for hands-on-experience.

The book is an attempt to share my experience in management over the years. To that extent this book is not in the mould of a classic textbook for study. Though an attempt is made to 'structure' the book somewhat, the information provided could be useful as a guide to improve a manager's effectiveness by honing his/her skills. The case studies and other material presented and discussed are real and so an understanding of these could prove advantageous to a practicing manager. However, no two situations are the same and so a manager has to be selective in applying a technique. One has to apply a technique that is 'tailor-made' for the specific application.

A fact that is turning out to be more important in these days of competition, both domestic as well as overseas, is the emphasis on the human asset. Employees are assets treated the right way. Man-management interface is the key to unlock the potential of the human beings that could be harnessed voluntarily for the overall good of the organization. That is the reason why a considerable portion of the book is devoted to the human capital and how this could be put to the best use through proven techniques. Delegation is the buzzword that could make employees feel responsible themselves and take up multi-tasking willingly. That is empowerment of the people in the true sense.

The culture of an organization is a factor that is assuming greater importance than earlier. There is a tremendous diversity in the culture within a country, and more so, while dealing with different nations. Since Corporates are going global, including a few Indian Multi National Companies (MNCs), the aspect of dealing with cross-cultural matters needs careful study and actions. That is a challenge as well as an opportunity for managers to interface with the managers and employees from a different cultural background that includes the language and behavioural pattern. Ethics in business dealings is a subject that needs careful and sincere attention. The public at large as well stakeholders could excuse a company for making an occasional loss but would never countenance a business that has adopted dubious and unethical methods to beat competition, cheat the government, treat the employees poorly and make a profit.

The book is divided into 11 major chapters and includes a Bibliography and an Index for easy retrieval of topics of interest. **Chapter 1** is "Introduction" that gives a brief history of ancient India and its values that included culture and management. The fact that some of the systems like the *Gurukula* and *Gharana* system work even now is a glowing testimony to the everlasting qualities of the highest standards in these institutions that continue to propagate education and art like music and dance. Indian way of yoga and meditation are briefly introduced that have influenced the world over drawing fresh votaries from different cultures. A few matters like leadership, teamwork, ethics have been briefly touched upon as introduction to these topics in the forthcoming chapters. "Management Tools" are discussed briefly in **Chapter 2**. There is no attempt made to cover each and every management technique. However, a few important tools are detailed that include: career development, communication, delegation, flexibility, recruitment, and training. Case studies are presented to make the 'tools' easier to follow and deploy, when needed.

Chapter 3 delves into the important topic of "Teamwork" that could make or mar the effectiveness of a department/organization. The manager/

leader has an important role to play in bonding between team members who are all supposed to work towards improving the effectiveness of the total effort of the team. A few individuals who might not work together harmoniously need to be handled differently. Cross-functional teams could handle inter-departmental issues better as individuals merge their identities for the sake of the target they have in mind. "Human side of the Enterprise" is about the human element in an organization that is dealt with in **Chapter 4**. An individual has ego, is sensitive to good and bad things and has a long memory especially for a feeling of hurt. That is the reason why a superior has to understand his/her people personally better for improved lasting relationship. One has to be a 'personal-touch' manager to vibe with the individuals. Managing people is an art and science where warmth of feeling towards fellow human beings could go a long way in improved workplace environment.

Chapter 5, "Promotions", is a discussion on using promotion as a tool of management to motivate employees. No other sops work as well as promotion, which means an improved status in the workplace as well as outside. This has to be done transparently, selectively and seen as fair by the majority of the employees, if promotion is not decided on an *ad hoc* basis. The craving for promotion is universal be it the lowly blue-collar worker or the CEO of a company. A few issues like managing disgruntled employees after promotions are announced are discussed. Attrition is a problem faced by organizations of any size. **Chapter 6**, "How to Manage Attrition", gives an insight into the various issues that are relevant to the problem of attrition. An organization has to re-orient their recruitment and compensation package to fall in line with the industry/business norms in any geographical area. However, those graduating from the B schools are a happy lot as some of them are offered plum postings with astronomical salary/perks. A few tips on how to engage the workforce and keeping them happy are discussed. Women employees need special attention and might need flexible-hours working where that is possible.

Change is inevitable and "Ushering in Change" is the topic discussed in **Chapter 7**. Organizations fail to see the need to adapt to changed circumstances that could prove costly. That applies to individuals too who have to become more knowledgeable, trained and experienced in multi-tasking. How to introduce changes that are acceptable to the majority are detailed. The change-maker has to do proper homework and learn to accept suggestions so that a change could be introduced with least problem. **Chapter 8**, "Organization", is about the various organizational structures that are being adopted to suit various business needs. Small business units are in vogue as there is quicker response and better accountability. MNCs are setting up their units in large numbers with their distinct organizational structure that ensures flexibility and quick decision-making.

Chapter 9, "Corporates" deals with the corporations, domestic as well as foreign, which have come to stay. These have to stick to set of regulations framed by the government on various matters such as pollution control.

They have a responsible role to play *vis-à-vis* stakeholders, public, NGOs and the environment. These important topics are discussed. A few corporations have taken social responsibility seriously that has spurred in improving the quality of life of their neighbourhood. The matter of ratings of companies is discussed that helps the public to know how each corporate measures by an independent assessment. How a corporate develops its culture is a matter detailed in **Chapter 10,** "Corporates and Culture", the penultimate chapter. Each organization tries to develop its own brand of culture over the years. Some are employee-friendly while others state they would support excellence. Others are good paymasters and most of them claim to do ethical business. The public knows a corporate by its support to a creed of excellence.

Chapter 11, "Future of Management", the final chapter delves into how a corporate could function in the future. This is something like crystal gazing and predicting the shape of management as science (and or art) in the years to come. A few fundamentals are unlikely to change-concern for customers, people, ethics and environment. Transparency in working of a corporation would be given greater importance. Recruiting and retaining talent are vital issues in the future where corporations would go global. Multi-cultural dealings would receive greater attention in view of globalization. Bibliography has a list of journals/magazines and books that could help a reading in updating his/her knowledge on management subjects of interest. This list is by no means complete or comprehensive and is given for guidance only. A detailed index is given for easy retrieval of key words and topics.

The subjects covered in the book are some of the important topics, which a practicing manager has to be knowledgeable. Case studies should help a reader to appreciate the nuances of any event. The names of persons and organizations mentioned are changed to protect their anonymity but all are real—either from the author's own experience or discussion with other company management experts and executives. It is hoped that the book would create interest in management subjects by those who are in business, managers and those who aspire to more knowledge. As such even students of management schools/colleges could benefit by the case studies presented and also by the discussion on various important topics. I have tried to share my experience in industry, business and consulting for the benefit of others. This might help a professional manager in getting a different perspective to the situation with the background presented in the book. However, one should note that no two situations are exactly identical and any tool/ solution deserves to be tailor-made to that particular case.

The subject of man-management is exciting with various possibilities of dealing with people whose only certainty is their uncertain pattern of behaviour. While there is no claim made that the book is a treatise on management, the topics and the case studies presented could prove useful to practicing managers, students of management and all those who are fascinated how a management works under different set of conditions.

Management practices have become more difficult and challenging in view of liberalization and globalization that have opened the world to freer trade and commerce, cross-cultural matters and a well educated workforce. The book is a small step in addressing such concerns and I hope it would serve its purpose of opening a small window to the world of management.

Bangalore D.B.N. MURTHY

Acknowledgements

Some of my management articles have evoked favourable response from readers, which gave me confidence that I was on the right track. That resulted in the book *"Of Man and Management"* which had good reviews in newspapers and magazines that went into several reprints. It is a pleasure to acknowledge the helpful comments and suggestions from the readers. Apart from such feedback, I had the privilege to interface with a number of management professionals, both domestic and foreign, too numerous to name. From my workplace experience I was fortunate to work and interact with some of the best management experts in the field who opened a window to the world of management. I was impressed by the emphasis of some of the CEOs to the important aspect of man-management interface. They emphasized the need for managers to have a heart and treat people with respect and consideration. Such advice has been a revelation when we think about tools and techniques of management bereft of the human element.

Certain business management magazines as also special editions of newspapers have highlighted management practices in the era of globalization, which I have found helpful. Internet is another source for valuable information on management practices and literature, which anyone could have access to. Some of the recent books on management, though on specific issues, as well as magazines and journals have proved valuable inputs to the book. I thank all these sources for the assistance I derived while writing the book. As usual my family has played its supportive role and also provided a few inputs that have proved helpful while writing the book. My sincere thanks to my family members who have been understanding and lending a helping hand when needed.

The publisher has done an excellent job of bringing out the book in record time and of good quality. But for the efforts of the publishing team the book would not have hit the stands so soon or of such good quality. I thank the publishers for their excellent efforts in publishing the book.

Bangalore D.B.N. MURTHY

1

Introduction

—The art of managing people

Management has been described as part science and part art. It is the ability to manage a team successfully that is the hallmark of a good manager. That person has perforce to lead the team from the front but give opportunities to the people to grow along too. Management of an organization is an onerous task given the external as well as internal factors in play. For instance, a manager might think that if the internal controls are in place and with a good team the organization could progress might miss some of the important issues that are external to the unit but important nevertheless. For example, the organization has to comply with regulations from various government and semi-government organizations to run its business within the framework of the rules set by regulators. The pollution control board might have fixed limits for water and air quality in and near the factory. The manager, especially the CEO, has to be aware of the pollution laws and take steps to control it within limits or else the unit could be fined heavily for non-compliance and in extreme cases face shut down too.

> Managing a nation, territory, city or an organization needs skills from the rulers.

Otherwise, if the administration adopts a *laisser-faire* approach, there could be confusion and chaos and normal life or work gets derailed. Thus, for an orderly conduct of life some sort of management is needed. Only under normal conditions useful and productive work take place. When the nation is under attack, most of the development work stops and the entire nation is geared to face the threat from outside. That applies to man-made or natural disasters, which ravage a nation from time to time. The immediate task is to rush food, cloth and medical assistance to the affected people as early as possible. Even a task of distributing food and clothes needs management skills so that there is orderliness in distribution, no wastage, no one is missed and no one grabs more than one's share and so on. Some of these skills are inherent and everyone does these acts naturally.

We have our ancient legends, like Ramayana and Mahabharata that speak gloriously about good management practices of our ancient kings and rajas. Some of them worked dedicatedly in the interests of the people under their care. The art of delegation was in vogue as the chief minister appointed by him handled the day-to-day administration. The king involved himself in a problem by exception. He was the sole dispenser of justice when every other channel failed to satisfy an aggrieved citizen. Feedback from the people was taken seriously and action taken to set matters right however unpleasant it could be. Justice was fair to one and all, high or low. Every action of the ruler was in the interest of the people he served. Taxes, if any, were reasonable and generally used for the benefit of the people. That some of them turned dictators and exploited the people for their personal gains is another sad story.

GURUKULA AND GHARANA

The ancient systems of education and arts have endured for centuries. In the *gurukula* system of teaching, the teacher took under his protection students from a young age who were taught not only the Vedas and scriptures but also martial arts, especially for the sons and relatives of kings and rajas. The students lived with the teacher and his family carrying out chores to help out the guru and his wife. There was total dedication and the students stayed with their guru for many years till the guru told them, "My sons, your education is now complete. You may go out and learn from any teacher or guru you like." The students gave the guru a parting gift as *gurudakshina*. This system has stood the test of time and nurtured excellence, a trait sadly lacking in our education system barring a few centers of excellence like the IITs and the IIMs.

The *gharana* system in music and dance is still continuing. The guru and his pupil have a dedicated relationship. The guru teaches the pupil all that he knows while the shisya stays in the same household devoting his/her time to learn music or dance. The various systems of music and dance have practically remained unchanged as distortion is frowned upon. However, there is scope for innovation within the bounds of the *gharana*. The *gharana* system is handed over from one generation through personal contact. That the *gharana* system, and there are several of them going strong, indicates the deep-rooted belief and conviction that this system is a good way of teaching students through a renowned master whose life is devoted to music or dance. Excellence is encouraged with little change from the original *gharana* style. *We have a lot to learn from such time-tested gharanas, which have created islands of excellence.* A bit of spiritualism in this materialistic world would breathe a breath of fresh air and provide the much-needed relief for the stressed human beings be it a CEO or a lowly placed workman.

Education of employees is assuming more and more importance due to rapid changes in the global scene. New technologies, new products, new processes and newer methods are emerging. Those who are computer savvy have an edge over others. Practically every employee, barring the lowest level in an organization has to be computer literate. Those in the R & D departments have to be abreast of the trends in the development field as newer developments are taking place on a regular basis. Even when employed, a person has to be abreast of the subject in his/her field. For this to happen a continuous upgradation of knowledge is essential to stay abreast of others. On-line courses are getting popular that enables a person do a course at his/her own available time. Distant education is a boon to those who want to work and learn at the same time. Apart from company sponsored training courses, the employee would do well to take initiative and join organizations, like quality control, human resource development, industrial engineering, chartered accountants and other trade associations, which cater to needs of specific disciplines. These provide training/seminars/workshops/tutorials/certification programmes tailor made to each discipline.

> Our daily life is full of instances where we apply management principles every now and then

We do not think much while applying some of the 'management' principles, which are partly acquired and partly inherent. "Common sense" is really an uncommon sense acquired by experience. For instance, we follow the people in a line while purchasing cinema tickets or while booking a rail ticket. We shop for 'deals' that give value for money. If the offer were 'buy two and take the third one free' most customers would buy at least two, provided they need such an item in the first place. They are pleasantly surprised they got a third one as a bonus. Another management principle people adopt is to make their life easier and orderly by opting for Electronic Clearing Scheme (ECS) payment. If a payment is due on a utility bill such as water, electricity or telephone, normally no user waits till the last date to stand in the line and pay for it. Moreover, smart customers use the services like the (ECS) to see the bills are paid directly to the utility company by the bank where the customer has his/her account. However, errors are not uncommon. So it is in the interest of consumers to check the transactions regularly and bring to the notice of the banks if any irregularity has taken place. *Caution is the word while dealing with transactions, which are not in one's direct control.*

LEADERSHIP

When it comes to managing an organization, company or corporate rules are different to some extent at least. The management has the onus of keeping the organization profitable from year to year just like households too will have to balance their domestic budget and hopefully put aside some money as savings for investment in real estate, children's education, marriage, overseas trip, medical expenses and other social commitments. The management team headed by the Chairman of the Board/Chief Executive Officer (CEO) with his/her team of directors and senior executives will have to devise plans to make the company profitable. However, considerations like customer focus, governmental regulations, employee's compensation, shareholders' demands, vendors' compensation, and other internal/external commitments have to be met honestly. No business could concentrate only on making a unit profitable without taking into considerations important factors, both internal and external, if the business has to last long. Management techniques are no doubt important to run a unit efficiently, optimizing use of resources, and for maximizing profit. However, these have to be considered in their holistic meaning so that vital factors too are considered while focusing on the need to stay profitable.

> A few gifted persons are born leaders. That quality comes to them naturally, be it to lead men or lead an organization.

For most of others leadership quality is an acquired skill. Perhaps it would be wrong to say that anyone can be a leader if he/she acquires the necessary skills. The fact is there are a few leaders but many followers. There is a special chemistry needed to become a leader of men. However, it does not mean one should give up on the quest of being a leader unless repeated attempts reveal that person is unfit to be a leader. That has been the reality when leaders of nations have floundered badly making a mess of a situation and had to be ousted with tragic results. On the business side too sacking of CEO, senior manager, or an employee is commonplace when that person fails to deliver the goods and the management has no choice but to show him/her the door.

> "The new century needs a leadership that is not subordinated to ideology but ideas." —*Aroon Purie – Editor-In-Chief, India Today*

ORGANIZATION

The trend nowadays is to make organizations lean and mean to take up challenges of competition head on effectively. The belief is that a shorter chain of command could take better and faster decisions. Moreover, even giant MNC Corporations have learnt a lesson that it is better to empower unit heads adequately so that urgent and local decision-making could be speeded up without involving the head quarters. Compared to the older organizations, the trend is to have smaller number of managers, who are highly qualified, trained and strongly motivated. That means their compensation package is much higher than ever before. However, it is the 'hire and fire' policy that prevails especially when it comes to managerial level appointments. Those who do not perform to the management's expectations are the first to be sacked when there is a downturn in the business or when the organization decides to get rid of deadwood without any hesitation.

Attrition in organizations is a cause of worry to some extent. However, there is a school of thought, which states a certain degree of attrition is good in the long-run as the company could hire more suitable people and also it could get an idea of the prevailing market position for availability of suitable candidates to fill up various positions as well as compensation package. A higher level of turnover could be a problem for any organization since it involves recruitment/training/induction with its related costs. Moreover, the smooth working could be disrupted, if the organization has to spend resources for the process of recruitment and training before the new recruits become useful. Organizations are concerned with the cutthroat competition in wooing the best talent such as graduates from the IIMs and IITs and other prestigious institutions. There is no denying the fact that a bright talented person is an asset to the organization and the investment in such a person is worth the effort and expenditure.

Induction of new employees is an important aspect of a Human Resource Department (HRD) function. Recruiting new employees due to projected growth, due to attrition or as replacement is an on-going exercise. This aspect is assuming greater importance. Campus interviews have become a standard format to attract the best talent from premier institutions. There is a virtual stampede to pick the best person(s) by offering huge compensation package unheard of in the past. Walk-in interviews, with or without prior appointment is another means of recruiting employees when the need arises. Advertisements in newspapers and in trade/business magazines is another means of attracting talent. The on-line talent hunt, through various websites of recruiting firms, is gathering momentum due to its sheer convenience and speed. By such a process it would be far easier to get a pool of suitable candidates, short list them and finally call them for test/interview, the whole process could be over in the matter of days, if the need arises.

> Training and motivation of employees, new as well old, has not received the attention it deserves

Mostly, the management thinks training and motivational programmes are non-productive investments and must be carried out somehow. Training managers are of lower levels compared to other departmental heads. They are often at the mercy of the powerful departmental heads who have the last say in the matter when, where and who would attend any training programme. A few 'important' employees manning vital functions cannot be spared by the departmental heads as the work would suffer. Induction programme, though so important to make a new employee feel at home and to learn more about the organization that person has joined, is hurried through from few days to one month at the most as the management is keen to put that employee in the slot he/she was recruited. "Ours is not a training institute," states a manager, with justifiable reason. Some employees get trained well but seek greener pastures soon after, as they are impatient to jump the line and leapfrog to higher levels with greater salary and compensation package. But others feel that the company that has trained them so well cannot be abandoned for short-term gains. However, they do expect to grow within the organization since the company has to have a career planning for each and every employee. This aspect needs to be carefully planned and executed.

Compensation package for an employee is a ticklish issue. For a new employee it is perhaps the single most important factor that determines whether he/she joins that company or not, other matters being more or less the same. How much is too much is an issue that could be settled by the market only. Certain companies follow the best practices and would like to remain in the upper range of companies that are considered good paymasters. Others try to match such a compensation package considered good but accept the reality that their resources do not permit hefty compensations to attract top talent. Another aspect that needs careful consideration is whether a new employee could be given a big compensation package that would upset the present loyal employees who have served the company well for years. These and more factors should be considered when the question of salary/perks/bonus/compensation are considered for new entrants as well as periodical wage/salary/perk revisions for existing staff.

TEAMWORK

Emphasis on teamwork is age-old. There is realization all around that no success could be achieved by one person in any endeavour, be it nation building, waging a war, or building an enterprise. People have to be harnessed into viable teams that work towards the objective. Training and motivation of members are important issues for the success of the team efforts. Coordination of such teams needs leadership quality from the person who is responsible for the team success. There is acceptance too that some teams achieve greater success than others. A healthy competition could spur the teams to work harder and smarter to gain recognition in the eyes of the management. Also, a point worth noting is that all members in a team do not contribute to the same extent due to inherent level of competence of individuals. These and more issues should be studied by the team leader so that he/she could prepare members of the team properly to meet the objective of the organization they are part and parcel of.

> The leader has the onus of convincing the team-members that the objective of team is to further the interest of the organization and not indulge in mutual bickering or one-upmanship

Rewarding teams/members is a sore point due to the fact that some subjectivity is inevitable. Such discrimination, knowingly or unknowingly, is a cause of unrest and unhappiness among the team members. They want to know the basis on which teams were rewarded and how these in turn allocated to individual members of the team. Openness and transparency in such dealings could go a long way in making the team members aware of the method of selection of a team as 'outstanding' and consequent award/ reward system.

CROSS-CULTURAL RELATIONSHIP

Many MNCs have set-up business in our country. Our businessmen too have set-up units in far away countries. The globe is shrinking with a plethora of mergers, take-overs and acquisitions. A new paradigm in business relations is taking place with many cultures and nationalities to deal with. This is an important aspect of the modern business trend with more to come as organizations are expanding due to compulsions of global free trade where the 'survival of the fittest' is the norm. Indian companies like Infosys are recruiting overseas candidates to work in their offices in India. That means we are dealing with not only Indians but foreigners too who have a different educational, family, and cultural background than ours. Unless a manager understands and appreciates the culture of the employee he/she is charged with supervision, that manager would have plenty of problems on his/her hands. This aspect cannot be brushed aside, as it is becoming more and more important due to the fact that free trade, commerce and employment are cutting across national barriers.

EMPOWERMENT

A few managers are worried about delegating/empowerment of their subordinates. The fear is due to the possibility of their losing control and authority over their people. They would like to keep the subordinates under their control. So, some of them take pains to curb a subordinate who is seen as a potential threat to his/her own position. That is a retrograde step and will not help the manager for long. That manager should have not only a broad mind but think of his/own position in the years to come. If he/she has to go up the ladder and assume higher responsibility, that person has to have the vision to develop at least some subordinate who could succeed him/her when the position becomes vacant. Making oneself 'surplus' need not be a traumatic experience as it benefits not only others but himself/herself too.

On the other hand, a few enlightened managers think it is their duty and responsibility to empower their people so that they could do their work better with less supervision or instructions. Multi-tasking is now taken for granted with educated employees joining the companies eager to learn and grow up in their career graph. Not only they are willing and capable of doing additional work but they demand such extra work/responsibility as they find that by getting trained early in their career their 'marketability' within and outside the organization improves.

In the past convincing an employee to do more than one job/task used to meet with stiff opposition not only from the individual but also from the employee/labour union.

The logic was by multi-tasking employment potential would reduce drastically. Moreover, they felt that employees were being exploited with little or minimal benefit to the individual. However, over a period of time individuals and unions began to see the point of view of the management. The threat of competition was looming large and unless productivity/flexibility increased there was danger of layoff, closure and lockout. It was in the interest of the employees that empowerment was accepted, though initially there was a mindset for any change.

Those managers who have perfected the art of delegation are a happy and contended lot. They have time to do their own work in peace. In contrast, managers who want to do everybody's work and supervise do not have time to do anything efficiently as they are always bogged down by routine and problems of their own making. *Delegation is an art*. There has to be mutual trust between the person who is delegating work and the one who accepts it willingly. This is a 'win-win' situation for both. The manager who delegates work has time to do his/her own work like budgeting, long-term planning, career planning for the people, attend useful meetings and be involved with other departments for mutual benefit. On the other hand, the employee who accepts delegation is looking for career advancement in view of the chance to learn and practice leadership quality and learn multi-tasking.

ETHICS, CONCERN FOR THE COMMUNITY AND ENVIRONMENT

Unfortunately, a few organizations have brought a bad name to business due to dubious and illegal practices. A few 'whistle-blowers' have done a great service by highlighting such illegal practices that enriched a few senior managers and directors. *Ethics in business is an important factor that determines the faith in that company by stakeholders*. They will not countenance anything that brings a bad name to the company of which they are the stakeholders. It is not only the CEO but also each and every manager and employee that has to conduct in a manner that brings credit to the company. Any tendency to cut corners or bend rules and laws should be nipped in the bud. The CEO should be a watchdog, with checks and balances so that the company is above suspicious dealings of any kind. Both the internal as well external auditors have the responsibility of highlighting unethical dealings and financial irregularities to the CEO so that actions could be taken against the culprits.

Concern for the community by a company is not new. The organization is a part of the community in which it operates. So it has to show concern to the development of the community by appropriate ways and means. Some organizations support educational activities, by funding schools in that area, others invest in improvement of the infrastructure, like roads that benefit not only the company but the community at large too. The neighbourhood families could also use medical facilities provided for the employees either free or on a small payment. Sponsoring cultural and sports events is another idea that a few companies have undertaken to give a boost to local talent, which also helps them to hog the limelight. A few sportspersons are on the pay roll of companies who have the freedom to practice and train during office hours. They are also encouraged to take part in important local, national and international championships. Indirectly, the company benefits by way of their support to sports-persons due to the 'visibility factor'.

Organizations have realized that they too should take a lead in employing physically challenged persons. Some of them reserve jobs for such persons who are as productive as able persons. That is a way of showing a company's commitment to help the challenged persons who deserve employment, not sympathy or doles. They have self-respect too and they should get opportunities to earn their own living in a dignified manner.

> Management is part science and part art. There is no set of tools that would make a manager successful.

One might learn various techniques in colleges and textbooks. The important matter is where and how to apply these. Thus the judicious choice of a management tool depending upon a specific application is what makes a manager successful. No two situations are similar. That is why one has to use a technique that is more suited to that specific application. Such judgment could be acquired through experience over a period of time.

An organization consists of human beings. The manager has to study this pool of human asset properly with the knowledge that they have emotions and egos. Anything that hurts an employee is a step back in improving relations between a manager and his/her people. *Trust begets trust and the more one trusts the people the better*. The days of strict and rigid supervision are over. Employees need space to grow and show off their skills and talents. Thus freedom as well as openness at the workplace is an important aspect that needs to be given careful attention by managers.

Innovation flourishes only when the employee has freedom to do what he/she wants to do keeping the overall good of the organization in mind. A friendly environment is conducive to improved relations between the boss and the subordinates. A manager should become a friend, guide, coach and philosopher to his/her people. That person might not be a fountainhead of all knowledge but certainly one with whom the employees feel free to approach with problems, criticisms and suggestions. Fortunately, Indian companies show more of their human face than their counterparts elsewhere and at the same time find the balance between profitability and social responsibility.

Inputs are getting scarcer and costlier. Conservation of resources is assuming greater importance than earlier. Gone are the profligate ways of running a business. Now the trend is to maximize the profit by minimizing the costs. That is the challenge for management around the world where competition is hotting up. Each company has to be customer-focussed so that it wants to deliver what he/she wants at an affordable price.

> Brand name is an important factor for not only buying decisions of customers but for those who want to invest in a company that has a good reputation in the market

Moreover, even vendors and employees would work with a company that is financially sound, has good sales, makes profits regularly and is environmentally friendly as well as sticks to ethics in business and in all its dealings.

> Management is above all an opportunity to serve the community by making profits but keeping the general interest of employees, customers, stakeholders, environment and the community in mind

A company should serve the community in which it is located as it has a social/community responsibility too. Managers should be smart and be visionaries to see the market trends in advance so that the company could stay ahead of the pack. They have to learn the management tools and use these judiciously. In view of the fast changing scene in the science of management, managers have to stay ahead by getting retrained regularly. They have to take courses on line as well as attend management-sponsored training programmes sincerely. It is necessary to be a multi-task person that would serve that person better either in the same company or outside, if the need arises. An employee has to become 'marketable' in his/her own interest by learning as many skills as possible. Keeping in touch with the latest developments in the field of interest, should be a regular task during the career of any manager/employee. Re-certification of professionals in a few disciplines is receiving better attention in view of the fast changing global trends and also opportunities to work overseas.

THE INDIAN WAY

We have taken much out of the experience in management from the advanced countries like the USA, Japan, Germany and the UK. In view of the global trends this is as it should be. However, in a few cases we have forgotten our own glorious achievements. For example, the *gurukula* and *gharana* system of learning under a guru has withstood the test of time. Westerners are flocking to India to learn more about the traditional system of holistic treatments of the human body. Yoga and Transcendental Meditation (TM) have caught the imagination of the world. Our Vedas and Baghavad Gita have enriched the body of philosophic knowledge the world over. *Spiritualism is gaining attention even in the business world*. That is because there is stress, anxiety and worry in this competitive world where everyone wants to go ahead, sometimes at the cost of others. We need to take a balanced view of life and understand that money, power and material comfort themselves do not bring happiness in individuals. There are a few higher matters that too deserve attention, for example being helpful to others, serving the cause of the community, working to conserve energy and the environment, and helping the disadvantaged and the challenged persons who too want to lead a life of dignity.

We Indians are basically individualistic and some of us find it difficult to work in a team. That needs to be looked into while harnessing people's power but recognizing individuals for their contribution. There are gems of wisdom available in our ancient texts on the art of management. We have to learn to use our Indian way of life like dedication to hard work, respect for elders and devotion to family to succeed in our vast country whose population has crossed the one billion mark. We have to have confidence in our ability to handle any situation to the well-being of our ancient land, which is slowly but surely turning into a land of opportunity for millions of our countrymen.

> "Connectivity will transform lives."
>
> —*Wim Elfrink, Chief Globalization Officer, CISCO*

2

Management Tools : Tools for Managers

—The right tool for the right application

A few managers think they can manage by 'common sense'. "Why should we learn or apply fancy 'tools', which are of no use anyway?" There is no substitute to common sense they aver. Some of them might be right. However, the fact is knowingly or unknowingly they would have used the time tested 'tool', which has come to them 'naturally'. There is another type of managers who swear by 'tools' that they have learnt in the class, through seminars or workshops or through self-learning. They are eager to show off their sophistication by using these techniques where possible just to impress others. The question arises whether the manager who swears by common sense for taking decisions or the one who cannot take any decision without recourse to a management tool is right. The fact is both of them are right to a limited extent in some situations. There is a place for common sense and also use of management techniques at the workplace depending upon any given situation. Moreover, that manager who thinks only common sense would suffice should think twice about his/her own effectiveness without the benefits of these tools that aid decision-making. That manager should appreciate the fact that the quality of decision-making would be enhanced if only he/she was aware of the array of management techniques/tools that could be used. Similarly, the manager who does not think of using his/her own judgment (common sense) to supplement the techniques/tools is well advised to do so.

There are many management techniques/tools available at the hands of a manager

It is like a box of tools with a mechanic. The only problem is that the mechanic should be aware of the right tool to use in any given situation as no one tool could operate under all repair conditions. Those who think a mere hammer or a screwdriver is enough to do any type of repair job are wasting their efforts in a non-productive manner. If only they had used the right kind of spanner or a wrench, the repair could have been completed within a short time and that too without wasting one's energy. That is the reason a manager's skills are known only when that person uses the right technique/tool to apply to a given situation. It is not that a tool should be used irrespective of its utility rather whether it is needed in any context. It is not important to know each and every management jargon, technique or tool. However, it helps a manager to keep abreast of the management tools that have been applied successfully by managers all over the world. Such knowledge would prove useful in the context of globalization, dramatic changes in the workplace, culture of the workforce, its expectations and innovations in technology, process, and material along with latest in HR (Human Relations) practices.

Some techniques (by no means exhaustive) are covered in this chapter. The idea is to expose a manager to some of the management techniques/tools found useful over the years at the workplace/office and which are still relevant, though with modifications/adaptations to suit a particular application.

> An innovative manager always looks for a technique/tool that is easy to understand and easier to implement.

That means he/she will not be interested in elaborate complicated techniques/tool that would need computer simulation and the like. There are time tested techniques/tools which have been found suitable in many applications. Any one could gain advantage by using these taking care to see that a particular tool is relevant to the situation on hand. In this fast-moving and changing world a manager has to focus on a few important issues as detailed in the Table below:

TABLE

- Hire and retain good people who could be assets.
- Understand key financial statements as everything ultimately boils down to rupees or dollars.
- Delegate work/responsibility effectively to the employees.
- Manage teams to deliver results by coordination and timely inputs of importance.
- Handle difficult and not so useful employees who could prove to be the drag for the team's effectiveness.
- Be pro-active.
- Deal with crises calmly and without panicking.

FLEXIBILITY IS THE MANTRA FOR SUCCESS

Much has been talked about flexibility in an individual and also in an organization.

The idea is that an individual has to be flexible enough to perform various tasks-longer or shorter working hours, flexible hours which means the person can opt for a timing suiting his/her convenience but taking care to put a few 'core' hours that are needed in the organization for contact, guidance, meeting the boss and colleagues, settling accounts, reporting on assignments in-progress/completed. An organization too needs to be flexible to operate under various conditions of demand. For instance, when the demand for a particular product is low, being seasonal, it has to be innovative in producing products that are needed by the market. That applies to quantities too—sometimes more and sometimes less depending upon customers' requirements. If a customer reschedules his/her requirements due to some reason, the producer would do well in trying to meet the new schedules willingly, to the extent that is practical given the constraints of procurement, scheduling, machines and processes and the like. However, compromises on quality are not accepted.

"No, that's not my job," is rarely heard these days, at least in the private sector, where the employees are supposed to be flexible and innovative. They are expected to be "jack-of-all-trades", though there is still a place for specialists and super-specialists in today's work-culture. That applies with equal force to whatever manufacturing/service an organisation may be involved in. In the past, organizations were churning out products or offering services because they were good at it, not because the customers wanted these. Such a phenomenon was not uncommon since the customers, by and large, were simply ignored. The producer/supplier/dealer had the (over) confidence they would find customers after their products/services were launched. Fortunately, such a mindset is slowly, but surely, changing. It is now the customer focus that is the primary consideration even before planning for any product/service.

One of the sound business practices of a company is its flexibility towards its customers. "But you had ordered a batch of 5000 pieces and now you want us to supply only 1000 pieces. How can we accept such a drastic reduction with just a week's notice?" is still heard from company's who respond, unhappily, to the changed needs of its customer. What such a company fails to appreciate is the fact that the customer, a long and loyal one at that might have his own compulsions, say, his own customer has reduced the off-take because it is not able to sell the product in the market. Who would like to stock items when the demand is low and might go down further due to competition or slump in the market? That could be the unhappy situation for a number of companies hit by diminishing markets due to recessional demand and when the economy is in a downturn mode due to various factors, internal as well as external. For instance, the slow down of economy in the US (2008) has had an adverse impact globally with a sharp nosedive of stocks in our country as well as impact on units that were targeting the US market for business.

However, a few organizations do not follow a policy of attracting and trying to please each and every customer. They 'prioritise' their customers for whom they might oblige flexibility of supplies. In other words, they might ignore a few customers whom they believe are not so important and worth all the trouble. "All customers are not the same," is the corporate philosophy of a few companies.

Those organisations that are capable of delivering what a customer(s) wants as and when he wants and the quantity of his choice, accepting changes after a reasonable notice period, are likely to stay in the market. A few companies have already benefited by the Japanese technique of "Just-In-Time" (JIT) system to work with low stock levels. A company that carries large stocks is losing money on those locked up unused stocks that are a dead loss.

> With the software packages that are available, some companies have streamlined their production process right from the planning to the delivery stage.

But unless the top managers are convinced that the customer is the king and that he must be satisfied despite any problem they might face, the organisation may not be considered efficient or customer friendly. Customers who are unhappy with their suppliers who do not respond to their change schedules might start looking elsewhere to get what they want. *Flexibility in operation is considered a powerful marketing tool in the face of stiff competition.*

An organisation can hope to be flexible in its operations only with the blessing of the top managers. But that's not all. Every employee should be motivated to adjust to the changed situation by being flexible. A prior condition is that the employees should have already undergone a multi-skill training and development where every employee is more or less confident of working with someone else's job, albeit temporarily. Moreover, the management, perforce, should create an environment that is conducive to inter-changeability. That can be done if the employees are committed to the organization's objective of satisfying the customers come what may. Such a situation is mandatory when there is a shortage of employees on any particular day due to any reason. By such a work-culture, rather difficult to introduce in any organisation given the mindset, there would be less excuses for failing to deliver the goods. Though absenteeism hampers smooth working, with multi-tasking matters could be brought under reasonable control.

It might sound strange if a management is urged to be less rigid and more flexible when it comes to handling its employees, contrary to the generally held opinion that strict discipline at the workplace is a must. For example, if an employee is allowed, as per the management-labour agreement reached every three or four years, to leave the workplace early twice a month, then there is no point in refusing that facility to an employee who requests permission to leave the premises early. No doubt, there are occasions when that particular employee might be requested to stay on due to the exigencies of work. But that should be an exception rather than the rule. *There is no point in showing off a manager's power to refuse.*

A disgruntled employee is unlikely to concentrate on his/her work.

That applies to granting of sick leave too. Employees are allowed to utilise, say, one week in a year as sick leave. It is the general experience that employees would like to keep that facility till the end of the year unless they fall genuinely sick. So everyone knows that the employee who reports sick in November and December might not be really sick. The manager in his enthusiasm to enforce discipline should not question the employee why he/she chose to fall sick.

"Millions of jobs in the manufacturing sector could vanish due to the dearer rupee hitting exporters across industries. Will things get worse before they get better?" (November 2007). It only means an employee has to be 'employable' with a wide range of skills that needs to be updated regularly in keeping with the times. Otherwise he/she would have a poor salability in the marketplace when it comes to a crunch situation. In fact, a few enlightened organizations think it is their duty to retrain employees regularly so that they are useful to the organization they are serving, and if need be, serve outside when it becomes inevitable.

TRAINING, KEY TO EMPLOYEE MOTIVATION

Training is generally a low-key affair in any organization given the fact it is considered inevitable but nevertheless a non-productive expenditure. The management wants the new employee to be inducted without 'waste' of time so that the organization can justify that person's pay and perks. "Why do you want six months to train the employee? Can't that person be put on the job within one month?" are some questions the boss might ask when a new recruit is put through the mill of training half-heartedly. Training equips a new recruit to know his/her job before being actually put on the job. That would form an induction programme for new recruits. However, if an existing employee is shifted to some other job, that person too should get an opportunity where he/she would be under training for some time before being made to work on the new assignment. That would help that person to familiarize himself/herself with the job for a sufficient period of time.

Some organizations put a new employee, especially a management/supervisory trainee, for an extensive training stint for 6 to 12 months before he/she gets a particular assignment. In such a case, that new employee goes through an induction programme, which is an attempt to equip that employee knowledge of several functions of the organization. Sometimes after initial training, the employee is asked to observe/work with an experienced employee who has been doing that particular work for a long time just to observe and learn the trade/task better.

Knowledge is empowerment.

There is no substitute to a good structured training programme as part of employee development right from induction through employment. This is no longer considered as "non-productive" expenditure as the effect of good training could reflect on the bottom-line in due course of time. Here are a few tips that might help an organization to make its training programme a success:

- Make it a planned structured effort not an ad hoc approach.
- Involve the employees fully in the training efforts by convincing them the need for training/retraining.
- Explain the nuances of any training method—the whys and hows.
- Demonstrate by practical examples what you have stated in words.
- Let the employees try with their own hands just to see how much they have grasped. Show then the ropes but not the noose.
- Before they go back to their place of work, give them an opportunity to watch senior (good) employees at work. They could get a tip or two from such experienced people.
- Let the employees try what they have learnt at the workstation. Watch how they do it. Correct any mistake they might be committing in the beginning when they put their skills to work. That is the time to see that they start on the right foot and do not make any mistakes or errors. Patience is the watchword when a new employee starts his/her work. Do not rush the learning period due to tight schedules and the like. Redirect the person if any lacuna is found in the work.
- Meaningful praise makes a difference to an employee who wishes that the superiors recognized his/her work.
- Do not order the employees to improve or else . . . they have to be convinced on the need for improvement. Respect begets respect and so treat employees as individuals with ego, emotion and feeling. Do not roughshod on those who might have not attained the right standards of work. You have to persevere with your efforts until improvement is brought about by constant encouragement and directing.
- Remind the employees: *"You can do it. You can do it better"*.

To learn new, first unlearn the old:

- Unlearn those skills, which are not relevant to the present scenario.
- Adjust to new work environment, new field, new technology, and new culture of organization.
- Unlearning is a challenge. Be receptive to new ideas, approaches and ways of thinking that are relevant.
- Acquire the capacity to learn new skills and knowledge.
- For some unlearning is a natural process to recondition old patterns.
- Train employees to set aside present ideas/practices that are no longer relevant.
- Internal job rotation where it is crucial to understand which part has to be unlearned so that the employees fit into the role.
- Unlearning is not easy when you are successful in the past.
- Unlearning is an attitude of mind. Training and coaching help this process.
- Expose employees to multi-skill jobs to facilitate the unlearning process and absorption of newer ideas, ways of working, change in culture of workplace and absorption of new technology.
- Conditional training methods to make unlearning easier.

"An individual has to see the benefits of overcoming the conditional and instinctive learning and reconditioning himself to acquire the knowledge required for the job. The training methods have to be holistic rather than focus on a particular area," avers a trainer.

RECRUITMENT

The Table below contains a few tips:

TABLE

- Learn some of the innovative recruitment practices in BPO industry
- Hunt for good talent
- Offer competitive compensation package
- Highlight the good PR of the organization and its ranking in the market place
- Give details of innovative packages that could attract and retain talent
- Give need-based training to new recruits
- Give a long-term view of the organizational strategy *vis-à-vis* employees

Skills desired by employers.

Here are some skills, which employers seek in new recruits:

- Soft skills
- Academic degree
- Aptitude
- Work experience
- Certified training
- Foreign degree

It helps to expose the recruits to some management soft skills like analytical methods, problem-solving techniques, communication skills, inter-personal relationship, teamwork, fast learning and customer relationship.

Furthermore, employers pay attention to a few more 'soft skills' of prospective employees that are listed below:

- Adaptability
- Can take pressure
- Creativity
- Analytical brain

Source : *The Week,* April 6, 2008.

CAREER DEVELOPMENT, A TOOL FOR ADVANCEMENT

Every employee has aspirations when that individual joins a new company/organization. Some of them set their sights high while others are more modest in their aspirations. While one might say to himself/herself, "Here I am as a management trainee. I hope to go up the ladder and become a departmental manager within the next ten years." The question is not whether such an expectation is realistic or not. The fact is the employee when he/she joins a new organization is fired with ambition to succeed. If on the way that individual realizes that the company's policies do not permit a new comer to rise so rapidly, that person would have made up his/her mind to leave that organization at the first opportunity seeking greener pastures elsewhere. Promotion, as we can see in a later chapter, is a powerful motivational tool. That organization which wants to retain a good employee would have made career planning an important component of its HR strategy. The fact is not every employee could be promoted regularly as that would devalue the meaning of promotion. It has to be selective but transparent so that every employee gets a chance to get promoted provided certain criteria are met.

Human Resource Department (HRD) does not get the attention from the CEO as production, R & D or Marketing. Often a person who is slightly below the rank of other departmental managers heads the HRD. While much importance is given to other functions, HRD gets a step-motherly treatment. It is considered an unavoidable appendage to an organization. However, organizations in the course of time have realized the need to upgrade the functions of the HR department and allocate it to a senior general manager/director. As such, career development of employees, from the blue-collar to the senior managers, hardly receives the attention it deserves which hopefully would change.

A new employee undergoes a brief induction training programme to familiarize him with the organization. Later on he is asked to attend a few training sessions/workshops/seminars programmes to upgrade his/her knowledge and skills. That should be a lifelong exercise and should be designed to keep the employee up-to-date on newer methods, skills and techniques. Of course, the employee too is expected to upgrade his/her knowledge and skills through own efforts.

> Career development is a structured approach to help an employee to help himself.

The training/motivational needs of employees vary from person to person. From the cynical remarks of a few managers, "Ours is not a training institute," we have come a long way in realizing the importance of training/ motivation in the career development of an employee. This is a proven management strategy for the overall development of an employee. If the employee improves, the organization benefits, such is the simple logic when an investment is made in a person by way of regular training and motivational programmes.

The first step in designing a tailor-made programme for career development of an employee is assessing the needs of such an employee so that he/she could contribute to the success of the organization. The best way is for the immediate boss and the next superior to interact with the employee every six months on a formal basis. However, one need not wait for six months in case something urgently needs to be done. The two-way communication is useful in highlighting the career development of a particular employee. While those in the management cadre have regular career development included in the six monthly/annual assessment, those in the non-management cadre do not get such attention, a real pity because even the blue-collar workers have their own aspirations.

Career development is a means by which an employee could hope to go up the hierarchical ladder. It is the management that decides when and where an employee would fit in the organization. Sometimes it is just a horizontal shift with different or added responsibilities. Such a move could be welcomed by an employee as it would improve his/her work experience and so his/her 'marketability' within or outside. The annual assessment is an indicator of the shape of things to come for the employee. "Mr. Sridhar could be promoted in the next two years," could trigger actions by the management to give Mr. Sridhar added responsibilities, assign him for management training or send him overseas to hone his skills.

The employee is often in the dark about his prospects in the organization he is working. Some of them do not hesitate to ask their superior what is in store for them. A few eager beavers might not wait for the 'normal' promotion time of, say, five years after joining the organization. Those who want to go higher up quickly do not mind job-hopping to improve their prospects. For such ambitious individuals, an organization might not have anything to offer, as any exception made would cause serious repercussions within. A certain degree of employee turnover is not unwelcome, as the organization as well as those who have quit may know their real worth in the job market outside.

"Ms. Shanta is too young. How can we promote her when there are other senior employees in the department?" could be the dilemma facing many a management. It knows that by denying promotion to Ms. Shanta they are taking a risk that she could quit for greener pastures outside. On the other hand, if the management promotes Ms. Shanta, though deserving, it could send ripples of unrest among others, which would be difficult to cope with. Dealing with 'high-flyers' is always a problem, which a management might not find a ready-made easy solution.

Career development is a useful management tool, which could motivate employees to give their best to the organization. However, if employees see that the strategy for career development is flawed, then it could act as a de-motivator as employees lose faith in such a system. *The career development programme should be fair and transparent as judged by most employees*. The management should involve the employee in his/her career development programme as far as feasible. If he/she desires to work, say, in the development department of the organization, efforts should be made to accommodate him/her in that department, subject to constraints. Instead of putting a person in a slot, it's far better to utilize his/her talents in the best way, the way that particular person desires. Unless there is a wholehearted commitment to a job, nothing worthwhile is achieved.

CASE STUDY

The assumption that only executives and white-collared workers aspire for career development is sometimes proved wrong. Ajay was an hourly rated inspector in the quality control department. He was a moody but very efficient worker who had created a good impression upon the fellow workers as well as the departmental head. In the annual increment/ promotion exercise Ajay was recommended for two additional increments. The boss called him to break the happy news. Instead of rejoicing Ajay was silent and looked crestfallen. The boss finally found out that Ajay was not happy with his hourly grade and so additional increments meant nothing to him. "Sir, with the additional increments my wages are more than the entry level salary of a monthly graded technical assistant. Why don't you fit me into the monthly grade with suitable slab adjustment?" he pleaded.

Ajay's request could not be met due to the fact that certain jobs, including inspectors, were classified as hourly rated. That was due to the agreement between the labour union and the management. The management could not change the *status quo* unilaterally. All that the departmental head could inform Ajay was that he was sympathetic to his request but due to the labour-management agreement he had no power to confer him the monthly grade of a technical assistant. Ajay was not convinced but reluctantly agreed that the departmental head had done his best. Fortunately, that anomaly was taken care of in the next labour-management agreement where some of the hourly rated jobs were classified as monthly. That meant a lot to a few employees who were more satisfied with the label rather than a mere wage hike.

An ambitious employee does not only aspire for going up the hierarchical ladder faster but takes concrete steps towards meeting his/her objective. Some of these steps could be seen in the Table below:

TABLE

- Set goals, as realistic as possible
- Create a good name by sincere and hard work without expectation of immediate results
- Attitude counts, be balanced and take disappointments in their stride
- Network with your superiors without trying to fawn on them but be dignified in your approach and do not attempt curry favour or be the boss (es) lap dog.
- Get smart about your moves that help to climb up the career chain. Do not miss opportunity when it knocks on your door.

CAREER OPTIONS

It is interesting to note what a new MBA graduate wants. A recent (2007) survey showed the preferred career options of MBAs:

Management consulting 37%; Investment banks/other financial organizations 29%; FMCG (Fast Moving Consumer Goods) 29%. *Source:* (*Business Today*, December 2, 2007).

RECESSION

Due to the global weakening of the US dollar (2007-08), and consequent appreciation of the rupee, our economy is in slight trouble. Export to the US has come down because of the downturn of the US economy.

> Millions of jobs in the manufacturing sector could vanish due to the dearer rupee hitting exporters across industries. Will things get worse before they get better?

SWOT ANALYSIS

There is nothing like 'self appraisal'. Who knows better an individual than the person himself/herself? To find out about one's strength and weakness SWOT (Strengths, Weaknesses, Opportunities and Threats) analysis helps as in Table below:

TABLE

> SWOT Analysis:
>
> Strengths:
>
> - What do you do well?
> - What is your USP?
> - What advantages you have over others?
> - What relevant resources you have access to?

RELOCATION OF EMPLOYEES

If an employee is a misfit in one department, he/she could prove to be a success elsewhere. The manager has to assess the employee's likes and dislikes and give that person an opportunity to prove his/her competence. Sacking should be the last option when repeated relocation attempts fail to enthuse the employee to give out his/her best for the organization.

TAKE CHARGE OF YOUR SUCCESS

Here are a few tips that could prove useful:

- Assess your strengths and weaknesses and identify personal vulnerabilities.
- Diagnose your situation and understand its challenges and opportunities.
- Negotiate a productive working relationship with your boss.
- Secure early wins that establish credibility and create momentum
- Build your team and connect with influential support coalitions.

—Harvard Business

COMMUNICATION IMPROVES MOTIVATION

A few managers and supervisors are surprised when some one tell them that they are poor communicators. In fact they are offended too. "I put up notices and I send circulars to each and every employee in my department. What more should I do?" they ask angrily. If you remind the manager gently, "But that's not communication" he/she would be bewildered and would be at a loss for words. What a manager fails to appreciate is the fact that communication is two-way and not just top-down. There must be a platform for the people who have received any communication to discuss and seek clarifications. Ideally, it should be a face-to-face talk with the person who is communicating. Otherwise it is nothing but an instruction from the top and no way is communication. There are practical difficulties when many people are involved for communicating. In such case smaller group, in each department could be called for discussion, exchange views and clarify.

The idea is to share information and to get the reactions of the people under one's control. By such a meeting it should be possible to apprise the higher-ups what the lower employees think and react to any matter of importance. Gone are the days of dictatorial rule while cooperation is in as this is the only way an organization could move faster. We have to take as many persons as possible towards achieving the organizational goal. If they all vibe together then even difficult tasks could be completed in time.

Two-way communication

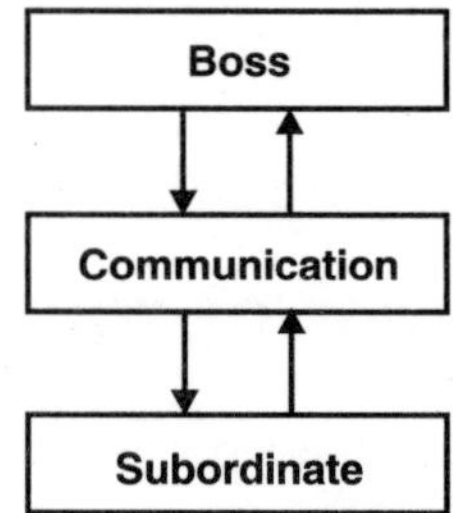

A manager should be open while communicating. Often the grapevine has a lead over 'official' communication. People already know what the official communication is and judge the manager for his/her frankness. If that manager tries to conceal something uncomfortable then the employees would jump to the conclusion the manager is less than fair and is not being truthful. The person who is in the process of communication should dismiss no questions as trivial or irrelevant. Otherwise the people would be afraid to ask any questions to save themselves from embarrassment. Some matters are company's policies, which should be made clear to the employees as that particular manager has little control over such matters.

> Information is power and a few managers think it is their exclusive privilege to have it.

A few of them are miserly about dishing out information with a fear that they might lose control over their people. On the other hand, like a sponge, they would like to absorb all and sundry information about others from their people. Such a double standard will boomerang on those who do not share information with others. For such managers 'communication' means keeping their people in the dark.

Some managers think putting up a notice is the end of sharing information. This is the 'communication' technique they are used to. Then there are those who go on sending small memos to their people believing that the more the merrier. They do not think what the recipients feel about such notes. Those who suffer from receiving an excess of memos eventually accept that it is part of the 'management' style of their boss and put up with these, as they dare not complain. Such memos, sent on matters of trivia or importance, fail to have any impact. There are managers whose telephone call is dreaded by the subordinates. Such a call is invariably to fire someone for an error of omission or commission. That is the sort of 'communication', which sends chills down the spine of the juniors. A few managers think they should call only those subordinates who have to be given a dressing down.

Communication is an art as well as science. One might know all the rules for good communication but fail to use these properly. Some are born communicators whose very body language impresses the subordinates. A few managers do not wait for a meeting but go around informing their people on matters of importance. That is the ideal manner of communicating, if that is feasible. That is because the person who receives the information can also ask for clarifications. People look forward to such interactions for mutual benefit and appreciate such personal touch.

> Communication empowers a person to make informed decisions and also enhance efficiency.

A formal or an informal meeting, preferably in small groups of about twenty persons, serves as a good platform to communicate, up and down. The manager might make a briefing and throw the meeting open for comments, criticisms and suggestions. He could then communicate with his superiors after getting a direct feedback. In a department, the manager or supervisor may have structured meetings with his people on a daily/weekly/monthly schedule. In fact, some of these meetings could be held in a conference room or even outside to make such meetings meaningful and in a relaxed environment free from the daily pressures of meeting schedules.

Each manager/supervisor has to develop his/her own style of communication with the people concerned. Without a proper communication the goals of the department/organization cannot be appreciated by everyone. *Complex matters can be understood only when there is a one-to-one communication*. The more time is spent on communication the better for improved understanding, cooperation and efficiency. People would like to know what is happening before a notice is put up or else they would get such information form the grapevine. Communication is a way of impressing upon the employees in an organization that the management cares for them and that they are treated as partners in progress. Such sharing of information, through a good communication system, is a sure way of bringing people together for the common good. That is certainly a confidence building measure as far as the employees are concerned. Thus communication serves a powerful motivator for the employees to give their best.

CASE STUDY

PRINT Systems was a small office working for an IT company. Sheela who was employed as a typist was worried that she would lose her job if she remained a typist, as she was aware that typists were in the endangered list of jobs. He boss, Suju, was an understanding person. "Sheela, it's better you learn more skills instead of being a mere typist. You have seen multi-tasking is the future for any person. It's better you learn the job of a telephone operator to begin with." Sheela was a smart person and willing to learn. She began to train as a telephone operator whenever she had the time. If the regular telephone operator was absent, she happily doubled for her, which gave her confidence. In the course of two years she had picked up the use of computers and instead of typing she used the computer to format letters. Suju was pleased that Sheela had learnt so much and that too with enthusiasm. In due course of time, she was promoted to the rank of a secretary. It just shows how the boss, if he/she communicates well and convincingly, could change the attitude of his/her subordinates.

DELEGATION

Delegation is not only a science but an art too! Some swear by it but a few others are scared of the thought of empowering their employees. "What if they succeed and I become redundant?" is the worry behind such hesitation in delegating work. There are some other managers who berate their employees. "What can I do? No one appears to be interested in taking responsibility. They are reluctant to take on additional responsibility," is their complaint. What they fail to appreciate is the fact that delegation cannot be thrust upon anyone. The ground has to be prepared so that the employees accept delegation/empowerment willingly. Employees resent the fact that their boss appears to them to be dictatorial. "Now from tomorrow you will take on this additional duty. That is empowerment, you know," he adds for clarification.

> The benefits of delegation/empowerment of employees are numerous.

First of all, the employees who are empowered are looking for a better career development, as they would be acquiring newer skills that would prepare them for taking higher skilled jobs. Moreover, it makes the employees feel important and they are convinced that is for their overall good. There are a few who are reluctant to take up delegation as they think they are being burdened/exploited with extra work with no additional pay or benefits. It would take some convincing that would clear the doubts of such people. Others willingly want to be trained and equipped with skills so that they are able to do the work without any problem. *It is the fear of failure that is behind employees' reluctance to accept empowerment.* "What will happen if I fail to discharge my responsibility properly?" is the worry and anxiety before accepting empowerment. Any manager/supervisor who is thinking of empowering employees should make it clear that he/she is there to help and not just to find fault. It is a good idea to have a trial period/run before empowerment is contemplated. That is the time where all doubts could be cleared so that empowerment is a success with least glitches.

Delegation helps employees to learn newer skills that would help them to go up the hierarchy. Employees need gentle persuasion to accept delegation and not through a fiat. However, the boss has to understand that if a subordinate is hard pressed for time, then it becomes his/her duty to help the employee out rather than tell the person 'It's your business." By such sharing of load, employees would tend to accept delegation more openly as they know there is someone higher up who is willing to shoulder part of the responsibility.

> But such 'upward delegation' should be an exception rather than rule as some employees could pretend helplessness though in reality that is not so.

CASE STUDY

The management of a machine shop decided that the lathe shop workers had free time and so they could as well inspect their products themselves rather than wait for the patrol inspectors to come and certify the products. The departmental head of the machine shop broached the subject with the supervisors. They were convinced the idea was good but hesitated to accept the new proposal as they too belonged to the labour union. "Sir, we accept your idea in principle. It is better you talk to the shop union assistant and the union leaders so that there are no hurdles in accepting the change." In the meeting with the supervisors, shop union leader and the union leaders, along with the HRD representative, it was explained by the departmental head why the suggestion was being implemented in the shop. "Competition is getting tougher and so we have to bring down the costs and improve quality. I can assure you the inspectors are being redeployed and no one is going to lose his job. Moreover, we are enhancing the wages of those who accept inspection as part of their job. We will give them training for one month in the use of inspection tools and explain the method of keeping records. For some time the inspectors would be going around the shop to help the lathe shop workers. We will give enough time for the workers to adopt to the newer method of working."

The introduction of the change was smooth and in about three months the lathe shop workers were fully trained in the use of inspection tools/record keeping. Not only quality but productivity too improved. The feedback from the customers too was positive. Thus the empowerment of the operators was successful. The lathe shop inspectors were redeployed as inspectors in another shop where there was a need for them.

3

Teamwork

—Mobilizing people

Much has been debated about teamwork, be it in business, sports or any other human activity. The idea is simple—"Two heads are better than one!" It is never a one-man show—even a brilliant business person or a shining sports star might not win on his/her own unless it happens to be a one-person business or sports like chess. Even then that person cannot do everything single-handedly, which is impossible. For example, a chess grandmaster takes the aid of his 'seconds', which helps him in formulating a strategy against an opponent. There are a few diehard individuals for whom working within the confines of a closed team is anathema as far as their creative development is concerned. "Why should I subjugate my creative skills in the larger interests of the team when I can achieve so much by myself?" It is a problem of integration of an individual with the rest of the team, which is the problem for some persons. Such individuals need counselling so that they try to work as a responsible team member in the larger interests of the team and the organization. Once they are convinced it would be in the individual's interest too to work within the team, they are likely to work with greater interest with full of energy to make the team effort a success. However, there are a few individuals who are misfits in any team due to their ego hassles and reluctance to work with others. Management should try a different strategy to utilize such talent.

Whether it is sports or business, teamwork is a sure winning formula for success. Where the members do not pull together, the teamwork fails to deliver the goods. Depending upon one or two "stars" may not be the best way of doing business or winning in sports. Just repeating the mantra of teamwork does not work. The members of the team have to be committed to the goal of the organization or team they are working for. A proper environment has to be created to enthuse the members to give out their best wholeheartedly. A mere fiat from the top management might not bring the team members together as people resent anything that is imposed from outside without their consent.

> Successful organizations have made it a point to select the right people who have a positive approach to teamwork.

A few individuals may not fit such group working because of their ego hassles or other personal problems. It does not mean, however, there is no place for such individuals who could work better where there is minimal liaising with others like analysts, researchers and auditors. However, it should be appreciated that the inability to get on with fellow workers is a serious drawback and the boss should try everything possible to counsel that maverick to change for the better. *No organization can afford to have too many such difficult individuals who have problems of interacting with others.*

Cooperation: Without good understanding and cooperation it would be difficult to make teamwork a success. This is one of the problems we Indians face from time to time. We are too individualistic which makes vibing with fellow workers a difficult task. That could be due to jealousy or mistrust. Such an attitude is in sharp contrast with the Japanese and other nationals who find teamwork the right way of working as a culture in the organization. Managers from time to time in our business milieu should emphasize the advantage of working together, if we have to mobilize people power to the maximum. The CEO and his senior executives should be talking and walking examples of good teamwork to be followed by others. *The culture of teamwork should be nurtured in every individual and encouraged to reach out to others*. For example, in certain organizations, every one is expected to suggest ideas for improvement. If each could contribute his mite, say, one per cent, then all these collectively could be a substantial figure when the sum total of all the efforts is collated. That is the reason why not even one small idea from anyone should be considered too insignificant to have any impact on the organization's bottom line. Little drops of water make a mighty ocean and the same is true of individual's efforts *vis-à-vis* team output.

Teamwork exists in a formal or informal way in an organization. Quality Circle, Group Activity, Small Group Activity (SGA) or Large Group Activity (LGA) are some of the formal groups for fostering teamwork. Also, a number of groups of like minded persons or disciplines exist in a non-structured manner—"Birds of a similar feather flock together." The idea of persons getting together is with the intention of tackling problems together, "Two heads are better than one." In all these groups, the paramount consideration is to pool resources together. Brainstorming becomes easier with groups with common goals. People come out with ideas and suggestions where they are likely to be heard and where persons are treated as equal partners within the group. That is why it is important for any person, however talented or brilliant he/she might be, to merge his/her identity with the group to make matters easier for others. Otherwise, there is a real danger that those who are not so gifted might remain silent spectators with a conviction that their views do not receive the attention they deserve. It is important too that not one individual dominates the proceedings because the others might not get a chance to give out their suggestions and ideas. That is why the team leader/counsellor/coordinator should control the proceedings so that every one gets an opportunity to speak.

LEADERSHIP

> The leader of a group can make or mar a team.

His dynamism can create the right wavelength for others to take part in the teamwork with enthusiasm. That is why he has to be careful not to be overbearing or be a mere spectator. People look up to him to utilize their services the right way for the well-being of the team. If for example, there is an expert in data analysis in the group, he should get an assignment that shall enthuse him. On the other hand, if the leader ignores that person's expertise and allots some minor or insignificant work, then his talent will go waste. The leader has the onus of giving the right opportunity for everyone to shine in the team. *The strength of individuals should be harnessed at the right time and opportunity*. We have examples in the sports field where the captain sometimes misses opportunities to give the right encouragement to some of his team members. The outcome could have been different if only the captain had given a thought to his strategy more carefully about each team member's strength and weakness.

Leadership could be as risky as it is rewarding and one has to minimize such a risk, to the extent that is possible. A person has to realize that a new leadership demands different skills. What is required is that the leader should focus on what it really takes to be successful in the new role, then discipline himself/herself, without forgetting the inner strength.

> Farsighted leaders have clear vision and strategy to plan for the future.

Here are a few tips for the management innovator as seen in the Table on the next page.

Managers should devise strategies to improve teamwork in the organization. They should convince their people the several advantages of working together for the good of the organization they are working. An environment of openness is a sure motivator, as the employees feel enthused to work for the common good. The less number of de-motivators the better for a person to focus on the job and give out the best. Otherwise it would

TABLE

- Expand management's sense of purpose
- Have revolutionary goals, but take evolutionary steps
- Make everyone in your company an innovator
- Guard against complacency, hubris, and denial
- Experiment, learn, Repeat

—*(From Harvard Business)*

affect that person's morale and attitude. Instead of concentrating on the work on hand that employee would be worrying about the de-motivators that hinder effective work output.

"The leader should leverage his understanding of critical issues to connect people across divides, while he himself communicates and connects with the diverse segments of society."

—*K.M. Birla, Chairman Aditya Birla Group.*

Such understanding is essential in this 'wired' environment where people from diverse cultures work together in a spirit of cooperation in the 'global village'. One needs to stay competitive in a fast-moving world by enhanced skill training through self-study/attending courses/seminars/workshops/on-line training programmes/courses.

CASE STUDY

The problem of scratches on the finished turntable was an interdepartmental problem plaguing a MNC company for long. The machine shop turned out parts, which were later on chemically plated by the finishing shop and delivered to the customer as a ready-to-use turntable. The major complaint was scratches, which spoiled the aesthetics of the part, which was visible. The blame game was endless—the finishing shop pointed to the machine shop for scratches, which in turn indicated the poor quality of the turntable blanks that were bought from a vendor. The packing and forwarding department also noticed there were scratches on the finished item at the time of packing. Moreover, the customer indicated that the packing too caused rubbing of the finished plates that created more scratches. Rejection at the customer's end amounted to an unacceptable 25 per cent and the customer threatened to cancel the order if the quality did not improve soon.

The Factory Manager called a meeting of all the departmental heads involved, including the Quality Department, which was responsible for the incoming as well as final quality of the product. He set-up a task force that included representatives of each of the department concerned, with the addition of the Process Engineering department that was responsible for the process layout. The team was given one month time to complete its study and come out with suggestions. The team started well by not asking 'who was responsible' but focused on 'what caused the problem' and 'what could be done' to prevent the problem. Various suggestions were considered after brainstorming sessions. The team worked as a cohesive one. At the end of the study various suggestions were put forth that could be implemented by the vendor who supplied the blanks and the other shops like machine shop, finishing shop and the packing/forwarding department which too were involved at various stages of manufacturing and packing. There was a dramatic improvement in the quality at the customer's end, the rejection being less than 2 per cent, which the customer accepted. It was indicated to the customer that the rejection would be even less in the coming months. Initially, screening at various stages for scratches resulted in higher rejections within but with proper precautions and care in handling, the internal rejection came down drastically. It was truly a fine example of a cross-functional team that could study and suggest ideas that improved the quality, bereft of inter-departmental squabbles. There was no attempt to point the finger at any one for the problem. *The sole purpose of the study was to improve quality through collective thinking and teamwork.*

EFFECTIVE BUSINESS RESULTS WITH AN ENGAGED WORKFORCE

A problem that plagues some organizations is the culture of 'groupism' that inhibits smoother cooperation. There is rivalry and bickering that could be unpleasant and not conducive to the growth of the organization. There is power struggle and unhealthy competition to be better than the other group. These groups are all 'unofficial' as people of similar backgrounds tend to come together as they think such an arrangement is good for them. That is 'teamwork' in the negative way since such groups tend to be exclusive rather than inclusive. They work for each group exclusively rather than for the general interests of the other teams, which would have helped the organization to pull together for better effectiveness. Some degree of 'groupism' or banding together of employees is unavoidable since 'birds of similar feathers gather together' as they feel each member could vibe with the others better. As such the background of each member is important in the group formation. For example, employees of an R & D department tend to be exclusive as they feel they are the real force behind the success of the organization.

> We should encourage cross-functional teams work together for betterment of the organization for which they are part and parcel.

The moment a team thinks it is superior and starts looking down on others as being less important then the seeds of non-cooperation are sown. For instance, packing is considered a low-tech low intelligent job and so best left to those who are barely literate. What the R & D people and even production people fail to appreciate is the fact that the packing department plays an important part in ensuring that a product reaches the customer in good condition. If there is a scratch or dent on the product or the packing box, the customer will not simply accept it. "Please show me another piece. This one has a big dent. How can I take it home when I have paid so much money for it?" would be the customer's natural reaction. The packing design itself may be top class but finally it depends upon the lowly paid labourer to put the packing materials in the right way and close the package. Suppose he forgets to include the technical literature and the guarantee card, the company is in trouble because the dealer would simply reject the package including the product as it is of no use to him. That is the reason why every department/team has to play its proper role to see that the product reaches the dealer/customer that is satisfactory.

The role of a leader over aeon has been discussed. But for the leadership role of such dynamic persons the course of history/business would have been different. The leader provides the vision, which is the catalyst for action that turns a particular situation to one's own advantages. It is clear not every one could be a born leader or made one through hard work and sincerity. Some think they have mastered the art of being a leader by looking and acting tough all the time to browbeat their subordinates. They only know a 'stick' to 'motivate' their people. Such motivation, if it might be called so, is inducing fear into the subordinates who dare not say anything for fear of being victimized. So they carry on doing whatever the boss wants them to do. However, their heart is not in whatever they are doing. Such work cannot result in anything great as the employees work without conviction because the boss wants them to do what he/she orders.

At the other end of the spectrum are bosses who are leaders because they want to get on with their people and motivate them to bring out their best. He/she becomes a mere facilitator for work. He/she is there as a friend, philosopher and guide when the employee wants advice, help or guidance. A leader has to remember he/she is one among the employees except that he/she is a coordinator and is not a boss just to supervise, threaten, chase and get the work done. *That is why a good leader trusts his/her employees and gives them freedom to work by their own initiative keeping within broad guidelines framed by the department/organization*. Much can be gained by the organization if there are committed managers who are leaders by their own right who could spur each employee to produce his/her best for the well-being of the organization they are part of. On the other hand, those managers who exert their might and suppress or even harass employees under them are doing a disservice to the organization as the employees work because they have to and not because they want to.

> Many of the turn-abouts happening in the marketplace is due to the leadership qualities of the top man who, often single-handedly, makes that vital difference to the fortunes of an organization in the doldrums.

One might be blessed being born a leader, for others it is sweat and inspiration with a slice of, what one might call, luck. A leader is powerful and with fortunes of many of his people in his control never loses that vital aspect of dealing with human beings—treating people like individuals. Even an unpleasant task, like reprimanding a person, could be done with grace and without bitterness, if the ultimate aim is to change that delinquent for a better person. Just like a ship cannot proceed without a competent captain, so too is the case of an organization which can muddle along facing roadblocks and floundering often without the guidance of a leader. No wonder then the headhunters are busy in fixing the right man for the right (top) job promising that person the moon. However, it is wise to remember: "Humanity flourishes in conditions made suitable by countless contributions from various quarters." No individual or organization could lay claim to being untouched by contribution of others.

A leader has some or all of the characters to be discussed in following paragraphs:

Patience personified: The leader is a person who oozes goodwill and bon homie and not one with furrowed brows and a stiff upper lip telling people that they are not welcome. A pleasant person has already won the battle of his people's minds. He has time for his people, barring exceptions, where he is handling a crisis or attending to matters of utmost importance. No one under his control needs to take a formal appointment with him. He preaches and practises an "open door" management.

Under such a set-up the people build a rapport with the boss who is seen as a human being understanding their needs well.

Openness: The workplace is not a prison where the people working have no voice. The boss, by his behaviour, will set the tone for inter-personal relations. He hears more and talks less. All ideas and suggestions from his people are given due consideration and credit while any idea, which is sound, would be accepted with thanks to the concerned person. On the other hand, more importantly, ideas, which are not accepted, would be discussed with those who have given such suggestions to explain the rationale behind their non-acceptance. We should remember that any rebuff by a boss is taken as personal insult and the affected person might withdraw into a shell. A boss might not only tolerate dissent by a subordinate but also would encourage that person to show dissent when needed so that ideas could go back and forth with the possibility of a better one to emerge. That contrasts sharply with the workplace environment where the boss acts like a dictator snubbing all dissenters to silence.

Responsibility: Sharing responsibility with others is anathema to some leaders who want to hog the limelight. Moreover, they are afraid that a junior person might replace him one day if that person grows from strength to strength. Therefore, he takes care to put that upcoming junior in his place and try to show him in poor light.

> People accept responsibility, and in a few cases, demand it too, given the right motivation and environment.

Recognition: Human beings crave for attention, whether it is home, sports field, art or business. It is not always possible to reward an achiever by monetary incentives or to promote him. All that person wants is recognition by the superior, and his colleagues, that he is a valuable member of the team contributing his best. Such recognition could be a mere handshake, a certificate of appreciation, a small gift/memento or just a pat on the back. While a manager is quick to reprimand his subordinate for anything going wrong, he is stingy with praise. *Praising an employee in front of others is a tremendous ego booster*.

Human development: With the installation of Human Resource Development (HRD) departments in organizations, more attention is being paid towards employee career development. Investment in HRD has improved training/retraining of employees, motivational needs and development of multi-skills. Development of leadership qualities too is given attention in order to recognize a talented person who could provide the much-needed leadership to a group of people. *A leader is always on the look out for any one who has the potential to blossom into a leader of men*. Thus, no effort is spared to give the much-needed impetus for leadership development, which is seen as an opportunity for better performance and not as a threat to one's own position.

Delegate: A leader does not try to do everything himself or enforce rigid rules for subordinates, which is irksome. Such a 'control' mania spoils everything as the people under that person resent the fact the boss does not trust them and so is at their back at each and every step. It is another matter if the boss wants to get periodical and timely report on the progress of work allotted to each employee.

It is clear in these days of liberalization/globalization, a leader who can make that vital difference to the organization's future is in great demand. The faith reposed in a leader is not misplaced as he provides the engine of power to the organization to excel itself. He is sharply focussed on the needs of his customers without whom the organization has no *locus standi*. By his persuasive manners, he wants to take the entire team with him because he knows the importance of all-round cooperation and teamwork.

> A leader, in contrast to a manager, is one who has the innate ability to thrive on ambiguity and dabbles expertly in managing paradoxes.

Leadership qualities could be acquired but one has to work on it. There are, of course, 'born' leaders for whom leadership comes naturally.

How a CEO or any manager makes effective use of the technique of time management determines how the organization progresses. Some of these are stated in Table on the next page.

TABLE

- Time management is an attitude, not practice
- Schedules with flexibility
- Prepare well
- Do have realistic deadlines so that there is enough time to complete the work on hand
- Self-development—know your strength and weakness
- Motivation needed
- Good feedback and support system

A sense of complacency could be counter-productive in the long-run, though the organization is charting a remarkable path. "The biggest enemy of great is good," says a CEO. It is said, "A good business follows the rules. A great one rewrites them, of course, within the ethical regime."

It is informative to know why leaders fail to reach their full potential. The following behavioural patterns were seen in those who failed as leaders: Imposter, rationalizing, glory seeking, playing lone, and being a shooting star.

Imposter: Believes in style, stunts and faking. They cut-off feedback channels and become political animals out to harm competitors.

Rationalize: Blame others and external circumstances.

Glory seeker: Some seek glorification and fulfil their own personal agenda.

Loner: Avoid close relations with subordinates and colleagues.

Shooting star: They are always on the go, travel needlessly, no time for family or friends. They have an early burn out.

Leadership in the digital age: We have now better educated and motivated employees joining the organization with high expectations. For instance, BPOs offer job/career opportunities to young men and women. After a while, they are likely to be disillusioned with the pay and compensation package, long unearthly hours but also limited career development. *It is for the leader of such a team to enthuse the employees*. No doubt high attrition is a reality of life given the fact that the youngsters are impatient for a faster growth and better pay and compensation package. Often the company's policies cannot be changed by the manager/leader but it is essential to keep the employees under his/her control happy, with the limitations imposed by organizational policies for which a manager has little control.

> Technology is changing fast and so it is necessary to equip the employees with the necessary knowledge and skills on a structured basis.

This is where a leader takes the initiative and recommends to the management training and reorientation courses for the employees regularly.

Not only such courses are necessary but also a leader has to pay attention to the interaction with the employees. Company picnics, outings, sports and cultural events help to break the monotony and are opportunities to get to know each other better.

> "The ability to formulate a shared vision of the world is the most vital attribute of a global leader."
> —*Mukesh Ambani, Chairman & MD, RIL*

Empowering people—A leader's perspective: Empowerment is a way of saying "We trust you." The more employees are empowered the better. A leader unsure of himself/herself is wary of empowering the employees in the department. There is a genuine fear such empowerment could mean the loss of his/her own importance. That leader thinks that if employees are given more responsibilities then this/her own position could be threatened and ultimately become redundant. However, a leader who is sure of enabling more employees has no such apprehension. There is confidence that with the empowered employees, he/she would be able to devote more time for long-term planning, career development of the employees, devote time for inter-departmental contacts and self-development. Empowerment does not mean the leader is free to do whatever he/she wants. After all, that person is still accountable for the work in the department. The higher management would hold the person in-charge of the department responsible for the results.

> "Some see the future, only a few make it happen."
> —*Teacher's Achievement Award slogan*

A manager has to be accessible to his/her workforce most of the time for guidance and leadership. The manager has to take time to interact with each employee and give feedback, both positive and negative, on the employee's performance. The idea is not merely to find fault but to effect mid-course corrections so that the employee is put on the right track. That is why there is little gained if the employee's assessment is held once a year to tell that person what went right and what went wrong. Yet such a yearly performance appraisal is needed for record and as a feedback to the higher levels to decide on quantum of compensation and career development as well as promotions and placement. However, the employee appreciates if the feedback is more prompt to him/her to effect improvement. Here are some tips about feedback:

- Praise a person in public but criticize him/her in private.
- Never shout at a person however much annoyed with that employee.
- Express your dissatisfaction in a dignified manner. Do not shout or use un-parliamentary words even in private. Blunt statements

and words hurt the ego of a person and that would rankle him/her for long.

- Be specific, with example, about the faults noticed and what should have been done in a friendly manner. Don't just brand the employee 'careless', 'not efficient', 'not focused' which sound too vague. Give recent examples so that the person concerned could relate to these events of the immediate past rather than something that happened six months ago.
- Explain what should have been done instead of generalizing statements like 'I don't like this,' 'This is not what I expect from you', 'You have not put enough efforts' and so on.

> The more specific you are in your suggestions/criticisms the better for the employee to understand and take corrective measures.

- Give clear-cut suggestions when you can to make matters clearer. Don't be vague about what the employee should have done under a particular circumstance.
- Find out whether your points have been understood by the person concerned.
- Your criticisms should produce positive results and so make it as less personalized as possible. *Point out to the problem and not the person.*

WHEN THE TEAM SPIRIT IS AT LOW EBB

A team beset with losses has a low morale. Not only the team members, coach, and owners but also thousands of doting fans are disappointed. They had high hopes of a creditable performance but the team has let them down. Hope gives away to gloom and those responsible for the failure of the team are identified and they would have a tough time explaining why their performance was not up to the mark. Those stars on whom the team hope rested are asked to explain why their performance was not up to expectations. The crowd might even boo some of them when they take to the field. This is not fair but given the adulation heaped upon them in good times, such disappointment in public cannot be helped.

The failure of our Indian Cricket team once in a way leads to low team's spirit. Given the fact that ours is a cricket crazy nation, millions of cricket lovers have high expectations from the team. They want their team to win every time they play a match. This is unreasonable but what can anyone do about it? It would be far better for the team as well as the fans to accept the fact that they are not the best. With such pragmatic acceptance, the team could hope to perform without high expectations or intense pressure. For instance, the lowly placed Bangladesh cricket team has done very well on rare occasions. On the whole, it loses to practically every team barring other lowly placed teams. In such a case, fans and others do not expect them to perform miracles. If there is a loss, and there could be a series of losses, they accept it stoically as part of life. They do not think the world has come to an end with such defeats. Some of the blame should go to the team captain but that is only part of the story. Unless every member feels that he can rise above his own self-set limitations, the team cannot do well. Similarly, a strong conviction is needed when the chips are down in business too. In fact, that is the occasion for everyone to pitch in his/her best instead of sulking or crying over spilt milk. *Enthusing team members when the going is not good is a matter of leadership.*

> Team spirit is not something one can buy. It is the sum total of all the convictions of the members of the team.

If a doubting Thomas thinks that the task given is too tough, the battle is already lost. On the other hand, if a member is so charged that he thinks he can do the impossible, some one or the other is likely to be motivated to follow suit. Just like negative vibes, positive vibes too travel fast. That is the reason why an optimistic approach is recommended instead of adopting a defeatist attitude. It is like losing the battle before even a single shot is fired. One has to have a strong conviction to succeed.

The onus is on the leader to inspire his people by his personal example. If a shipment is due next week, he simply does not sit in his office and order his workforce to work harder. He is ever present on the shop floor to straighten the bugs but does not like to step on the toes of his subordinates. He is not a master chaser but a facilitator of work. If over-time is needed, he stays back and works shoulder to shoulder with his people. Such a camaraderie is what the employees want when the going is tough. They are sure that with such active participation of the boss matters will be sorted out faster in case of problems.

> A leader might not be a fountainhead of all knowledge. As such, he does not pretend to have all the answers to the questions of his people. He is honest enough to admit that he does not know but could arrange to get some one who is likely to have the answers.

Such openness, instead of lowering his esteem in the eyes of the subordinates, will enhance it for being so honest and straightforward. They will think that he is after all human and not a demi-god to be worshipped. *The more honest and open he is with his people the better for enhanced team spirit.* Every individual has the capacity to excel himself. He is pleasantly surprised that he/she had so much reserve energy waiting to be tapped.

To rebuild a team is an opportunity as well as a challenge. Not surprisingly, one man could prove to be a catalyst in inspiring the entire team. Suppose the leader tells his/her team: "Look friends, we are all here to sink or swim together. Let us believe in ourselves and give our best. Let us put the past behind us and start a new chapter in the life of the team. Let us remember that no one could inspire us but ourselves. An outsider could only be a guide or catalyst to help us to help ourselves." However, often mere words of encouragement are not enough to make a team tick and show better results. Here an expert/adviser/consultant could prove useful in identifying the strengths and weaknesses of any team, be it in the sports field or in business. What is needed is a good interaction with the consultant who should have an open mind. Every case is unique and so there cannot be a cut-and-dry solution. The consultant cannot behave as if that person knows everything and others are there just to follow the advice. His very attitude to the members can make a difference between success and failure of the efforts put forth by the consultant.

CASE STUDY

A new CEO of a MNC company had taken over. He was informed that due to governmental regulations further growth would be difficult. There was a brainstorming session in which the new CEO took an active part. He raised several interesting points, which made the senior members of the management team to think over. "Let us find an 'out-of-box' solution," the CEO exhorted his colleagues. At the end of the meeting there was no light at the end of the tunnel. The CEO was disheartened but didn't give up his efforts to find a solution to the present deadlock that had impeded growth of the company. In the next meeting, after several futile discussions, the CEO had a flash of inspiration. "Why not take up branding of products in a big way? Are there restrictions on getting products manufactured by our qualified vendors and then brand it as ours?" he asked. The team members were pleasantly surprised that a novel idea was thrown upon which details were worked out. It was confirmed that branding to improve sales/profits was acceptable and there were no legal hurdles to such a scheme provided the parent company took full responsibility for the product quality, including after sales service. That was the beginning of a new chapter in the company's growth graph that saw healthy sales and profits in the following years.

4

Human Side of the Enterprise

—Dealing with emotions and egos

An organization consists of people, which obvious fact a few managers sometimes tend to forget. They are more concerned with buildings, gardens, transport, machines, finance, stocks and so on. People are not only taken for granted but considered as unavoidable expenditure and so the duty of any manager is to get the maximum output from each employee while paying the least. The axe falls on the human being in times of poor results and continuing recession. A manager does not think or feel too much while informing the employees under his/her control that "lay-off has become inevitable and so they need not come to work from the next day." "Of course, you will get half the wages/salaries," that manager adds gratuitously. Such is the kind of treatment a human being gets while working in an enterprise. However, matters are slowly, but surely, changing as the Chairmen/Chief Operating Officers (CEOs) have begun to realize that without total commitment from their employees, all innovations, product/process improvements and expectations of higher turnover would come to naught. You might have the best of technology, up-to-date processes, latest machines, and excellent systems and procedures but without the willing and wholehearted cooperation of the people working in any organization, the results would not amount to much.

The CEO sets the standard how the organization deals with its people. There are enlightened CEOs who feel people come first, technology and process later. Such people-centric organizations have an edge over others where people are taken for granted. Involvement of the employees is taken to greater heights as the CEO feels that people have to be taken into confidence at each and every step. Take for example a case where an organization is facing stiff competition and there is no alternative but to scale down the wages and salaries at least temporarily to tide over the immediate crisis. A day would come when the next month's pay bill amount might not be available due to paucity of funds, a cash crunch situation, and so the organization might have to skip that month's wage/salary disbursement. Desperate situations call for desperate measures. The CEO calls a meeting of his senior managers to explain the awkward situation and he urges them to convince the people under their control that they should cooperate with the management to tide over the crisis.

Contrast such a scenario with an organization where the CEO is concerned with his/her image and wants to have his/her way. That person wants to act tough and wants to make sure his/her tough stand would be appreciated. Such a person would simply inform the senior managers about the crisis and ask them to accept salary cuts voluntarily to set examples to others. Then he dictates a notice to be put up on all notice boards that the organization would reduce the salary/wage due to 'unavoidable' reasons. It would state further that if the situation continues to be difficult then the next month's salary/wage might have to be deferred. The employees would fret and fume at such a bombshell and wonder what sin they have committed to face such a financial crunch. They grumble that in good times, the managers get all the benefits with little trickling down to them and that too after pleadings by the employees/labour union.

It is not enough if the Chairman/CEO is employee-friendly and has a 'human face'. Such an attitude should trickle down to each and every manager and supervisor. Unfortunately, some organizations have delegated dealings with the employees/labour union to the Personnel Department now generally labelled Human Resources Department (HRD). So the managers refer each and every employee-related case to the HRD, acting as mere postmen shuttling the problem either up the hierarchy or to the HRD. Such a way of working makes the manager removed from his/her own group of people who look to him/her as a father figure to help them out. Such managers would lose respect from their own employees if solutions were found elsewhere without the active involvement of the manager concerned.

> That is why in some organizations, they expect each manager to be his/her own 'personnel manager', referring or consulting the HRD only when needed.

However, managers are expected to find solutions themselves within the broad framework of the set of guidelines each organization would have framed. The fact is a manager is supposed to work with his/her employees day in and day out and so is expected to know each employee better than anyone else. Each individual's strength and weakness are supposed to be known to the manager (immediate boss), which should facilitate understanding and with that finding a reasonable solution to employee-related issues is possible. Nevertheless, a manager has to be careful in promising something he/she cannot deliver as that would affect adversely that manager's credibility. In such a situation, he/she should take time and consult the next higher level of management and also the HRD before making a commitment.

THE HUMAN FACE OF A MANAGER

Those who manage people have to understand human psychology. A stern face will put-off people. The subordinates may not appreciate the fact that beneath that stern visage of the manager lies a soft heart. A cheery "Good morning" could do wonders. It will immediately build that rapport so essential for smooth working. That people should leave all their worries and anxieties at home is easier said than done. Every individual is a human being with problems both on the home front as well as at the workplace. That manager who appreciates such a fact would do everything possible to put the employee at ease though he might not be able to solve all that person's problems. The interpersonal skills of the manager are called upon to assuage the feelings of the subordinates who want a shoulder to cry on when they are in difficulties. If an employee has a sick child on his hands, he expects the boss to be understanding and allow him to take leave while showing his deep concern. Managing people is different from managing other resources like finance and technology. It is more of an art than science. *People have long memories for both good and bad things.*

A few managers want to appear important. So they seldom come out of their offices. If someone wants to see him, that person has to take an appointment with his secretary. Similarly, he sends words through his secretary to the person concerned to see him at a designated time. That is too formal and inhibits close and personal contacts between the manager and his people. Contrast such a style with a manager who believes in managing by "walk-around". He sits in his office for a short time to clear files, attend meetings and handle confidential matters. But most of his time he is seen at the workplace talking to the people or seeing for himself how things are being managed. He gets firsthand information of the problems faced by his people and offers solutions, if he knows them. Otherwise, he promises help through others. There is an air of informality about him.

> A manager who is informal has an edge over another who believes in managing by fiat.

If a boss comes around to a place of work, the person behind the machine or equipment is open about his problems. On the other hand, if a manager hardly visits the shop floor or workplace then he has to get information through his supervisors that is often biased. Often a simple problem gets out of hand if tackled late or through supervisors instead of by the manager himself. *A personal rapport between the employees and the manager through direct contacts will stand the organization in good stead.*

In case of labour-management conflict, that manager/supervisor who has established a personal rapport with his people is better-off. People respect him, not as a manager, but as a warm person who can vibe with them. Consequently, they might appear lukewarm to any proposal from the union or anyone to harass the boss. They might go about it half-heartedly, telling the manager that they are helpless but will not do anything out of the way to embarrass him.

A walk-around manager will not claim to be the fountainhead of all knowledge and expertise. In fact, he could respect any employee who tells him what to do in any ticklish situation. At best, he is a facilitator of work, skilled in interpersonal and intra-personal matters. He would not do anything that might lose trust of his people. He could be a tough taskmaster but a warm-hearted person when it comes to dealing with the people working with him. He will never ask a person returning from his sick leave why he couldn't have come back earlier. He sympathizes with the personal problems of his people when he comes to know about these. He might not solve all their personal problems but would lend a shoulder to cry for a disturbed person.

> There is everything to gain by being a personal-touch manager rather than a tough looking, tough acting boss.

OVERCOMING ONE'S OWN LIMITATIONS

It is said, "Man can move mountains," in a metaphorical sense that a highly motivated man could do wonders. Each individual has set his/her own standard for performance depending upon that person's self-interest and degree of motivation. But a change is possible if the individual is convinced that what is good for the organization is also good for him. For instance, a boss might tell an employee, "Please attend a seminar because it will be good for us." Mentally, he would weigh the consequences of attending such a seminar. He would, in general, conclude that such an exercise would add to his bio-data and so improve his marketability. On the other hand, if a suggestion is made he should undertake a week's fire-fighting course, the reaction is predictable. "I have to attend the course otherwise the boss might get upset. Anyway, this is a course I am not interested. What's the use of such an exercise that won't help me?"

The work-culture in an organization determines how the employees react to any suggestion. It could be a place where challenges are accepted willingly because the environment is conducive to it. For those who are in the thick of a battle to meet newer challenges, it is excitement and a joy working towards their goals, however tough these might be. The reason is obvious—they want to excel themselves on an ego satisfaction trip. The individual is fully committed to the goal on hand and is sharply focussed on it. That is the big difference between self-motivation and the one where the individual is forced to work despite his misgivings. In such a case, one could be sure that there is no wholehearted commitment to the task on hand. He would simply do what he is told.

It is the mental barrier that is the bottleneck to one's own capabilities. If an individual is convinced, rightly or wrongly, that he is capable of so much and not beyond it, nothing much could be done to change it except through repeated counselling and through peer pressure. Once he is prepared to overcome his own self-set standard of performance in whatever field that individual is able to perform much better through training and motivation. *Such is the power of persuasion, not coercion*. Once a person achieves a higher set of standard, for example, he can turnout 100 pieces of production instead of 80 pieces per hour through improved method and through self-motivation, he could be expected to perform even better. Of course, there is an upper limit for any performance. For instance, not every chess player could expect to become a World Chess Champion like Viwanathan Anand despite that person's total commitment and efforts.

However, a word of caution would be in order. The management cannot expect an individual to go on improving day after day until he/she reaches a higher level of performance if at all he/she is capable of achieving.

> There is a plateauing of performance beyond which even incremental improvement becomes very difficult.

Moreover, the individual is worried that he/she might not be able to improve continuously due to various constraints. And, more importantly, he/she has every right to expect something in return for all the improvements he/she has achieved. If there were a labour union, it would put brakes on an individual's desire to improve. It would think any productivity improvement is a matter of discussion between the management and the labour union and that a management has no business unilaterally asking an employee to work beyond a set standard of productivity norms already agreed upon. Thus, any improvement plan might have to be worked out in cooperation with affected individual and or labour union.

To make a person rise above his own limitations, real or imagined, is not easy. He has to be convinced that it is possible to do so and should be shown how he could do it. The tools for realizing an improvement have to be provided and the person trained to apply these. That is not all—there has to be an incentive for trying to achieve a better performance. Constant encouragement is needed to see that the person carries on bravely despite setbacks and failures. The colleagues in any department should have a helpful attitude so that the person trying to excel himself is not isolated or that person becomes a butt of ridicule or, in extreme cases, ostracism. The person who has succeeded after a string of failures is a happy and satisfied man. A mere pat on the back for a job done well is sufficient encouragement to that person though incentives like money, gift in cash, kind, additional increment(s), and promotion are significant indicators of the management's appreciation. *Such recognition could serve as a powerful motivator not only for that individual but for others too.*

> An organization consists of average employees with a sprinkling of bright talent, which is always in short supply. The challenge before a management is to motivate the employees, targeting the average ones, so that they rise above their own self-imposed limitations.

Then only the potential of all the employees is fully harnessed for the good of the organization. *It is amazing how ordinary people could do uncommon things when they have the right motivation*. It is this potential of employees that is waiting to be tapped by a responsive management who see the people as real assets. The people should share profits and receive awards/rewards in recognition for their efforts to make the organization grow from strength to strength.

> Seeds of success—belief in yourself.

"We want passion for our business. Workers who can interpret and execute our mission, who want to build a career, not just take a temporary job." —*Howard Schultz*

If you perform well, you become a good employee and an asset.

A few points that merit attention are indicated in the Table below:

TABLE

- Dress well and properly
- Follow rules that are made to bring order into the system
- Take responsibility for mistakes. Do not hide or make others scapegoats for your own mistakes
- Be considerate to others besides your own self-concern. Be a good and active team member
- Develop communication skills
- Take on-line training modules to improve your skills
- Respect and cooperate with your boss
- Try to do the job on hand with efficiency and sincerity
- Be punctual. If you have to absent from work, inform your boss in advance or as soon as you can
- Try to work without much supervision or guidance. Take pride in your work and see how to improve your efficiency.

- Accept responsibility willingly and voluntarily
- Be a friendly man to your subordinates and see that they can approach you anytime for any problem. Keep the channels of communication open up and down
- Do not misuse company's time, products, and services for your personal use
- Think what you can do to make yourself more valuable to your organization

Every employee is supposed to know what's expected from him/her and see that this is accomplished to your own as well as your boss's satisfaction. Try to vibe with your boss as well your colleagues. Find out discretely what they think about you and your contribution. Make suitable changes, if possible, to become a better team player. The boss expects you sometimes to become a leader, innovative and creative. Whatever you do should inspire confidence in the boss and rest of the team members.

Be eager to shoulder any responsibility smilingly and without ifs and buts which is a sure means of going up the ladder of success.

You are expected to be a brand ambassador of your company. That means you are supposed to know your company's products, services, policies, ethics and all that. It is also important to know what your competitors are doing in your line of business. An aspect that needs emphasis is the need for an employee to stay physically, emotionally, and mentally fit by proper diet, exercise and relaxation. Spend enough quality time with your family too. Be dignified even when you make adverse comments about your organization or boss. You must enjoy your work and do not consider this as a nine to five daily chore to be completed somehow. The more jobs you learn the better as you would then fit anywhere as a multi-task person. Your worth within the organization as well as outside would then improve considerably. *Exhibit a positive work culture so that the task on hand is completed efficiently.*

MANAGING PEOPLE

One of the most unpredictable species is the Homo sapiens. One moment a person can be the most reasonable one and the next moment he could be roaring like a tiger on some trivial issue. Thus managing the human asset is perhaps the most challenging job of a manager who is expected to deliver the goods. Unlike a few cult figures, he cannot turn employees into zombies to work at his behest. At best he can threaten, coax, cajole or appeal to their better senses to work for the good of the organization.

One-to-one contact between the employee and his superior on a regular basis, formal and informal, goes a long way in removing misunderstandings and to build a bridge of understanding. Often, a small issue is blown into a big controversy, which could be avoided if there is a personal touch during the interface between the two. It is possible to sort out problems during the interactions rather than sending notes to the concerned or hauling up the subordinate for some real or imaginary breach of discipline. The subordinates will have to realize that they and the boss are working for the same organization and so they should pull together. Barring minor irritants, it should be a smooth sailing if the superior has an open mind while dealing with his/her people. When a subordinate is faced with a ticklish situation, he wonders why the boss had not briefed him about that matter, which would have cleared the air. Thus, openness in relationship could go a long way in easing workplace-related tensions and problems. The manager has to be employee-friendly to get the work done by the employees and to create a bond between him and the employees. A stick or a threat is no more a 'motivational tool'.

How does one make an employee feel part of the organization? First of all the manager has to be sincere, in his attempt to involve the employee in not only day-to-day work but, as far as possible, in planning and decision-making at least in that person's sphere of work. That means the manager leaves the employee space to work out for himself. He is there to guide and coach him.

> The less supervision the better as an employee might feel irritated by too many instructions and follow-up to the point the employee is fed up with such an intrusive approach by the boss. The employee is hurt that the boss does not trust him.

Here are a few tips how a manager could build rapport with his people:

Delegation: The quantum of delegation normally depends upon the capacity of that person who is willing and able to take up responsibility. Not all employees could be burdened with work or responsibility since they are not capable of. Some of them have to be trained to take up a responsibility and should be assured that delegation is not only good for the organization but for the employee's career graph too.

Communication: Information flow up and down to an employee tends to be scarce. There is no two-way communication with the boss who generally keeps the information to himself. Sharing information may make an employee feel part of the organization. He would rather get the needed information from his boss directly rather than through the grape vine or from a notice. He then feels important that the superior has confided him.

Compensation: This is a matter to be decided at the highest level of the organization. However, an employee would like to know why a certain compensation has been fixed the way it is. He is none too happy to hear, "But that's a matter of policy." Being open about even management policies will certainly strengthen the employee's feeling that he is being treated as a person. He might not agree with the package offered but at least he is aware of the background.

Openness: Gone are the days, hopefully, of a bureaucratic approach to human relations. It would be taken for granted, in the earlier days, the subordinate would follow whatever the boss tells him to do without questioning. With a better class of employees, better educated and experienced, the boss is no longer an autocratic ruler whose word is law. More employees are asking the boss why a certain matter has to be dealt with the way he thinks it should be done. Moreover, it can happen that the employees are more knowledgeable about the latest developments than the superior is. Therefore, it helps smooth working if the manager is patient, open and willing to listen and act upon the suggestions by the employees forming the team. They would appreciate a manager who shows willingness to change rather than stick to his decision as a matter of personal prestige. He should work like a coordinator rather than a superior person up the ladder.

Tapping talent: Making employees entrepreneurs should be on the top of any manager's agenda if he wants to make his team dynamic and make them accept challenges enthusiastically. The organization should be able to tap the potential of the employee and give opportunities for him to rise above his own self-set limits. *Each person has a body of knowledge, skills and capabilities waiting to be tapped.*

Career development: Managements have not realized the need for careful planning of an employee's career. It is either *ad hoc* or just a routine exercise. An employee hopes a management would take care of his growth needs. Moreover, the employee expects that he would be given the much needed training/re-training to carry on his job or any other job more efficiently. With the growth in information and technology, an employee needs tailor-made programmes to enhance his skills. Such a development augurs well for the employee as well as the organization by enhancing that person's 'marketability' within or outside. Promotion is one of the most under-utilized tools and a management would do well in putting in place a sincere and transparent promotion policy which is seen by the majority of employees as being fair and so something to be aspired to. 'Promotion delayed is promotion denied,' and the management cannot keep a person on the tenterhooks by denying his promotion indefinitely. That is certainly not motivation!

Dealing with high-flyers: An organization cannot have all genius type individuals, as the supply is limited and erratic. These mavericks, "wild-ducks", are highly imaginative and very impatient. They do not believe in 'normal' work or 'routine'. They tend to make rules rather than follow rules. Such people could be assets, treated the right way, or could be thorn in the flesh of a management. These high-flyers are dynamic individuals who are often obsessed by their own self-importance. However, they have ideas, which look so much out of the way and 'out-of-the-box' that it could sound very novel and ingenious. Even one or two ideas and suggestions from such individuals, if implemented, could transform an organization into a dynamic one. Nevertheless, the price might be high to retain such mavericks.

> Managing people at best of times is difficult given the individuality of the people, their likes, dislikes, ego hassles, emotions and aspirations.

Dealing with the variability of human beings requires not only skills but also human understanding. "Stick" or fear of punishment is a powerful de-motivator. In sharp contrast, praise and sympathy for an individual could be the bonding necessary to get the best out of an individual. It is no more fashionable to assume that a manager is a fountainhead of all knowledge and so the people under him should obey his instructions blindly. With better-qualified and experienced employees, the boss has to hone his interpersonal skills to cope with a variety of situations while dealing with human beings. *Thus, managing people is more of an art rather than a science and those who empathize with their people have a head start.*

> "Leadership needs spiritual intelligence."—*Danah Zohar,* Thought leader, Physicist, Philosopher and Author.

AIMING AT PERFORMANCE EXCELLENCE

In these days of tough competition, from domestic as well as International players, an organization has to be on its toes and watch the competition carefully. There are several matters for the management to attend to and take action so that it is in a good shape to take on the competitors. Some think that by improving technology they could find the market friendly. Others lay stress on their human resource development. What is important to understand and appreciate is that the organization has to show an all-round improvement if it has to survive. For instance, if it improves the production process but fails to improve its marketing and service areas, customers are not impressed. They would go in for suppliers who could meet their requirements faster, better and at affordable prices.

A few of the factors that an organization has to work and achieve improved performance are listed below:

*Customer-drive*n: It might sound elementary that an organization survives because it has customers. However, a few of them still behave as if it is a protected market. Their attitude towards customers of 'take it or leave it' is the real hindrance to their progress. Each and every employee starting from the CEO down to the lowly helper has to focus on pleasing customers, in order to meet the goals of the organization.

Continuous improvement: What was good enough yesterday might not be enough today and certainly not tomorrow in view of market trends for improvement. *Status quo* is taboo as the customers expect better value for their money in terms of additional features or improvement in performance at the same price. That is why organizations have set-up quality/productivity/safety improvement teams whose objective is to lay down, implement and monitor improvement in parameters of products/services which concern the customers the most. *The culture of improvement has to become a way of life in an organization where everyone strives to improve upon past performance.*

Employee participation: It is the people in an organization who have to improve too not only machines or technology.

> The employees should be trusted as valuable members of the team whose willing participation in every affair of the organization spells success.

They need periodical training/re-training/skill-upgradation as well as the right motivation in view of rapid changes in technology, machines, processes and methods of work. People have to be empowered too so that they could take up additional responsibilities wholeheartedly.

Fast response: A factor which is not receiving much attention is the quicker response to market demands. "We cannot supply that item because we have to re-set our machines and processes. Let the customers wait for a little longer," kind of responses are no longer acceptable. If an organization cannot supply, others are waiting to fill up the vacuum.

> Once a customer loses his trust and confidence in a particular supplier, it would be difficult to regain it. It would take then greater efforts to woo him back

Flexibility: Along with fast responses, flexibility in operations is vital for survival. If a customer wants a, say, 5 pieces of a particular product, he should get it without much delay. Then only he would have the interest to go back to that organization for a repeat order or for a new device. Flexibility in operations means the organization is tuned to the customers' wavelength and not merely interested in delivering what it has produced.

Results oriented: At the end of each quarter, it is the bottom-line that counts and not what the organization has achieved in terms of, say, employee training and development, induction of new process, lowering of stock, though each of these factors are important. Some managers are obsessed with techniques as if these are the be all and end all of matters. One has to focus on results without compromising on the integrity of the process/product/service. *There are no short cuts to achieving results.*

Leadership: The top managers have to be talking and walking examples of leadership that could make a big difference to the fortunes of an organization. The leaders inspire their teams who in turn are enthused to be part of an exciting journey towards excellence. Merely paying adequate compensation and expecting employees to work with their heart and soul is asking for too much. They need a reason, apart from money, why they should work so hard and what is there in store for them when the organization makes a handsome profit.

Corporate responsibility: An organization should be known for its ethical products/services. At the same time, the stakeholders would like to be associated with an organization, which has a social responsibility towards its shareholders, employees, vendors, government, NGOs, the environment and the public. The image will suffer if under-the-table dealings are indulged in for short-term gains. Meeting pollution standards, not using child labour, and employing persons with different abilities are other social factors of concern.

ENSURING EMPLOYEE SATISFACTION

"Our first step towards customer satisfaction, employee satisfaction," states the corporate policy of Zuari Cement Company. It further says, "We prefer calling them partners, rather than employees. Partners in progress, to be precise." A few such enlightened companies treat their employees as valuable assets rather than mere wage numbers. The reason is simple—employees should feel part of the company. For that to happen every employee has to be free from worries and tensions, as far as possible. Then only each employee could give out the best towards the welfare of the company of which every individual is part.

> The company might not solve personal problems of employees but it would at least provide them basic needs and, more importantly, a workplace where there is an environment of freedom. It should be a place where it would be a joy to work, instead of it being a mere chore.

It might not surprise anyone that an employee in a company, which is paying well and is a stable company, might desire a change. *He would rather work in a place where he is recognized as a person with emotions, feelings and ego.* Thus, the working conditions play a vital role in an employee's desire to give his best for the team. That just does not happen by chance. The superiors have to create a conducive environment of *glasnost* where dissent is not only tolerated but also encouraged. The boss is not some stiff character sitting in his air-conditioned office, but one who is more of a friend, guide, coach and philosopher. He is there to lend his shoulder for a junior to cry on, when it comes to that. He is not a master chaser but one who is a facilitator. He might not be a fountainhead of all knowledge but willing to admit his errors of omission and commission and is willing to learn even from his subordinate. Thus, the people working in his team see the boss as someone to be approached who could help when the need arises.

The more responsibility an employee gets the better for his self-development as well for building confidence in his ability as a multi-dimension person. A company has to think and plan the career development of each employee however lowly he is. Rotation of jobs and developing multi-skills are assuming greater importance in view of an open market economy. The trend is to have smaller viable units, which are lean and strong. This means each employee, as far as possible, is trained to handle a variety of jobs to increase flexibility, which is nothing but 'multi-tasking'. Employees who work and are trained in such a company are grateful that their "marketability", both within and outside the company has improved.

Much has been talked about a "compensation" package, which depends upon the paying capacity of an organization. Those who promise a high wage and other benefits might not be able to keep such promises for long. On the other hand those who pay as per the industry/area-wise norm are in a better condition to continue such wages and compensation package. What an employee looks for is stability and continuity. Often, an employee wishes for a promotion rather than higher wages. That is because promotion is an eye-catcher and an attention getter in the organization and outside. A company, which has a better plan for career development of employees, including promotional prospects, has a definite edge over another, which is stingy about promoting an employee.

> Attracting talent and retaining them is a matter of deep concern for any organization in these days of intense competition. Several factors work in *employee satisfaction index* and so an organization has to innovate to keep abreast of techniques, which enhance employee satisfaction. "We care for you," should be a strong message from the CEO.

Bob Nelson, President of Nelson Motivation Inc.

Nelson's Top 10 Recognition Factors are given in the Table below:

TABLE

- Support and involvement
- Personal praise
- Autonomy and authority
- Flexible working hours
- Learning and development
- Manager availability and time
- Written praise
- Electronic praise
- Public praise
- Cash or cash substitutes

EMOTIONAL ENGAGEMENT AT THE WORK PLACE

"Please do not bring your family problems to the workplace," admonishes a manager to an employee beset with his personal problems. That is easier said than done. If someone is not in a good mood, is tense, anxious and in fear, anger or sorrow, it is difficult for that person to concentrate on the work on hand. Emotions do play a major part in a person's concentration and work. This aspect has not received the attention it deserves. A manager cannot solve domestic and family problems of an employee. Yet he could be sympathetic and try to understand the problem and do whatever that is possible under the set of given parameters.

Let us take the case of an employee whose spouse is unwell. That means the employee has to spend more time at home and the hospital caring for the spouse. In such a case the superior cannot be heartless and say, "I don't care what happens at your home. Please be regular in your attendance. You are taking far too many leave of absence." The manager might be right as the work suffers but what can the hapless employee do? Moreover, such an unsympathetic attitude could cast a shadow in the relation between that employee and the boss. Even other employees, who are not directly concerned with that individual's problems, won't appreciate the attitude of such a boss who appears so heartless.

CASE STUDY

Vasan was a senior manager in a private company. He got a call from home at ten in the morning informing him that in far away Kerala his father had died suddenly that early morning. He had to rush back home to take part in the obsequies, as he was the eldest son. The moment the CEO Rupa heard the news, she ordered her personal assistant to see that the company provided the needed facilities and that Vasan was given all the assistance required. Two seats were booked on the emergency quota on a flight from Mumbai to Kochi and an office car was put at the disposal of Vasan and his wife to reach Mumbai in time to catch the flight. Fortunately, they could make the flight and reach Kerala well in time for the funeral.

The above was by no means unique for that organization. Even for the blue-collar workers a similar treatment was given. After all, the company could not prevent deaths and other family events but surely it took the lead in seeing that all assistance was given without delay and hesitation to rush succour to the affected employee. In case of death of an employee or his near and dear ones, the organization had made it a policy to rush a senior manager along with adequate funds to pay for the funeral and other expenses as well as render all possible assistance to the bereaved family. That was a way of showing to the employee and the affected family, "We still care for you!"

COUNSELLING

> A few employees, whether one likes it or not, fall a victim to drug/alcohol abuse. That affects adversely that employee's quality/quantity of work besides endless sickness/family-related problems and frequent absenteeism.

There are friendly counsellors, who are on the panel of a company, who could assist the employees to kick their drug/alcohol problem. That needs patience and understanding and not any tough act such as "mend your ways or face sack!" Often the immediate family members of the affected employee are taken into confidence before any such counselling would start. Unless the family members too cooperate it would be tough for the employee to get de-addicted to the abuse of substance/alcohol. Nowadays smoking ban is in place at the workplace, which is causing problem to some of the employees who are compulsive smokers. They too need help in minimizing the effect of such a 'no smoking' ban at the workplace.

A person who is constantly anxiety ridden, angry and depressed needs the help of counsellors, the family as well as co-workers to become a near normal person. That is not easy given the fact that such an affected employee might not be aware in the first instance that he/she is showing signs of depression, anxiety, fear or anger. In such a case counselling becomes more difficult, if that person does not participate in the counselling exercise willingly with a view to return to normality.

> Such counselling need not be a traumatic experience for the employee or his/her family concerned provided a degree of confidentiality is maintained.

If need be, the affected employee could be advised to admit himself/herself into a de-addiction centre to hasten the process of rehabilitation. Such an event itself should not be a black mark on the employee provided he/she shows improvement after a period of treatment. In fact, such employees once de-addicted could become productive once again.

5

Promotions

—For one's ego trip

"Promotion is the most underutilized tool," state Tom Peters and Nancy Austin in their book, *A Passion for Excellence*. The question is often asked why it should be so. The boss who has an able assistant wants that person to grow up, but not too fast. The fact that he/she had to wait for a long time colours his vision. There is reluctance to see any one growing up faster. At the back of the mind is a nagging worry, "What if the assistant goes up too fast and starts posing a threat to him/her directly or indirectly." That would be one of the reasons for the boss to decide to chart out a slow and steady progress route for his/her assistant. By such a 'proven' strategy the manager sees safety not only for the person concerned but personally too.

Those who get promoted early and frequently do face problems not only for themselves but from others too. Some of the favoured ones feel so important that they start thinking they have become indispensable and might throw their weight around much to the annoyance of colleagues and higher ups. People, in general, do not like someone who is arrogant and drunk with power. A degree of modesty would serve such a person well though a few jealous colleagues cannot stop wagging their tongues and telling others juicy stores, mostly fabricated out of malice, how that person managed so many promotions within such a short time.

Every human being seeks recognition, be it the humble daily blue-collar worker or the CEO of a company. Each in his/her own way contributes to the well-being of an organization. The least that person expects is a suitable reward. Despite cash and other incentives, promotion is still regarded as the most suitable method of recognizing the contribution of an individual. For that very reason, a promotion policy has to be fair, free and open but selective too. Otherwise it loses its charm and meaning. If all the executives are told during the annual appraisal, "From the next financial year, all of you would be designated as team leaders with a substantial hike in pay and perks. Your designation would be senior managers." That, we think, is sweet music to the ears. However, more than half of them would say to each other, "What's the big deal? There is no meaning that all of us are re-designated but that is no incentive at all. I wish the company were selective and promoted only a few of us."

There is expectation from an employee that the management would take care of his/her career graph. The time for appraisal, once in six or 12 months, is for stocktaking, both ways. The employee, after an assessment has high hopes as the meeting could have gone off well. It is but natural for that employee to feel elated that the manager had given an indication that he/she is of a promotable material.

> No manager should hold out high hope or promise for an assistant's promotion since uncertainties are involved.

"You promised me a promotion but you have failed to honour your commitment," could be the outburst of a dejected employee when the promotion list does not contain his/her name. This is but a natural reaction and that cannot be helped. Nevertheless, the manager could assuage the feelings of the aggrieved employee by explaining various factors that are involved before an employee gets promoted. "I have done my best," could sooth the ruffled feelings of the person who is cut up as he/she failed to get promoted. Yet, as far as that employee is concerned, the management has not been kind to him/her for bypassing his/her case.

GOING UP THE LADDER

> The intense desire to seek promotion is universal.

A daily-wage worker wishes he could become a monthly wage earner though it might not mean much as far as take-home wage is concerned. A middle manager aspires to become a departmental head with all its perks and responsibilities. A director of a company has his eye on the managing director's slot because he thinks he will become his own boss. Such is the strong desire of individuals hoping to climb the hierarchical ladder in an organization. In most government and semi-government organizations seniority, by and large, is the criterion for promotion. Thus a few brilliant individuals have to wait for a long time to get their just dues. Any out-of-turn promotion causes a problem, often with judicial intervention to restore the *status quo*. There are administrative tribunals who too take up grievances of aggrieved officers in government jobs.

CASE STUDY

Mohan was a Technical Assistant in the incoming inspection section of the quality control department. He had reached the highest level in that grade T4 and he had no further avenue for growth. The only way was to promote Mohan to the officer grade M1, which was proving difficult, as the job was not classified to be a M1 level post. However, he was not convinced that nothing much could be done. What he wanted was to climb the hierarchical ladder and how that was done was not his problem but that of the departmental head. Mohan used to sulk for one week despite counselling by the departmental head whenever management promotions were announced. The departmental head tried his best to convince the higher ups that Mohan's post needs to be upgraded as he was entrusted with important decision-making on goods involving thousands of rupees. Finally, the factory manager was convinced and his case was recommended. Mohan was overjoyed when the departmental head handed over the promotion paper the following year.

It is worth noting that Mohan's take-home pay as a T4 as would have been higher than as a M1, as per the labour-management agreement that was finalized that year, but yet he gladly accepted the management position as it satisfied his ego, bettered his prestige as well as his personal standing in the factory. That applied to the home front as well with his friends and relatives. That's the charm of a promotion, though sometimes financially it might not benefit the person that gets promoted due to pay-scale difference. The fact that he would be getting less than a T4 didn't dampen the enthusiasm as it meant several intangible benefits-separate transport, canteen, and no clock punching. The management realized that the recent promotees needed to be compensated in view of the latest wage agreement. Mohan was more than pleased when his scale was revised so that he would get a higher salary than a Technical Assistant in the T4 grade.

"Oh, he is too young. Let him wait," is the general remark when a bright young spark is being considered for a promotion. What managers fail to understand is the keenness on the part of talented youngsters to go up in an organization as quickly as possible. So they do not subscribe to the management policy of "wait and see" but would like to be promoted whenever and wherever possible irrespective of the number of years they have put in or the number of seniors who are in the line of promotion. If they do not get what they want, for them the lawn is always greener on the other side and so they do not hesitate to change jobs. The word "loyalty" has no strong meaning for those who have self-interest above that of the organization they are serving. *There is more mobility in the jobs now than earlier*. That makes job-hopping easier, however, with the inherent risks involved in such changes.

> A management confronted with the need to utilize promotion as a tool for motivation has to do its homework properly.

The promotion policy has to be open, honest and merit-based as seen by the majority of the employees. Just one wrong case of an undeserved promotion could put a permanent black mark on the organization's promotion policy and that might become a (wrong) precedent too. If an out-of-turn promotion were given, due to some reason or the other, the majority of the employees would be very unhappy and they have every right to question the management's action. That's more so when an employee secures a promotion by devious means such as "blackmail" by waving the offer of a competitor. It would be better to let such an employee go, though after trying to persuade him/her to stay back, rather than pander to his/her demand that could damage the credibility of the management beyond repairs. It would shatter the morale of a large number of employees by just trying to retain one individual, by hook or by crook, however valuable he/she might be. The echo of such a cave-in by the management could be heard for long and could become a dangerous precedence.

There is nothing like anyone being 'indispensable' as someone or the other is likely to fill up that vacancy. Moreover, a certain amount of employee turnover is inevitable and could prove useful in getting to know where the organization, and also the employee stand in the job market. That could prove a blessing in disguise too as fresh talent could be inducted for the sake of infusing young blood. At the same time the organization could benefit from the exit of an employee who is ineffective as well as uncooperative, a poor team player at that. That doesn't mean, however, the management should not talk or try to persuade that individual to stay back without promises that cannot be fulfilled. An exit-interview could reveal facts more than that meets the eye as the individual could throw some interesting facts why he/she is leaving the organization. Such a feedback could be useful in re-setting the course of the organization *vis-a-vis* the job market.

A FAIR POLICY

Not everyone could be promoted in an organization as otherwise that management 'tool' of recognition/reward will lose its meaning. There has to be a premium for good and smart work. An individual's contribution should be evaluated objectively. A recent incident should not cloud the boss's opinion about his subordinate who otherwise has done well. "His work needs to be watched," could put a spoke in an employee's personal record and might jeopardize that person's chance of promotion.

> The boss should not be vindictive because he doesn't like someone.

On the other hand, a boss might be critical and demanding about an employee's work but when it comes to pushing that person's case for promotion, he could be enthusiastic. Anything put in black and white in a confidential report (CR) could mar that person's future such is the power of the boss over a subordinate. As such the boss has to be careful in what he writes. On the other hand, he should not hesitate to find fault, give instructions and occasionally take him to task, if there is something lacking in that employee's work. The boss has to realize his responsibility towards all employees under his control and care. That means the boss has to be seen as being fair towards all and has malice towards none. However, he could be tough with the people without being harsh or unreasonable. *The boss could be a tough taskmaster but at the same time a coach, guide and a friend.*

"If we go on promoting everyone where do we have so many positions or posts?" asks a senior manager. There can be only one head of the department, only one factory manager and one managing director. Promotion causes joy in one person but heartburns in many that cannot be helped by the very nature of promotion that is selective. After a while, especially in older organizations, a time comes where the slot for promotion is limited. Unless there is diversification or expansion, employees have to accept the fact that the organization has not many openings. A situation of 'Plateau' will occur in course of time and employees might have no further scope of going up. It is the skill of the managers how they deal with such persons who might lose interest and motivation to work, as they see no light at the end of the tunnel. *The older employees feel neglected that should be a cause for concern for the management*. These people may be old but are loyal and have the maturity to stick on irrespective of the ups and downs of the business cycle. They are valuable employees who have to be treated with respect and consideration. They are certainly not deadwood to be treated with disdain. Even an old dog could learn a trick or two, if the master is imaginative.

CHANGED SCENARIO

> Promotion policy of an organization should reflect on the management's concern for efficiency and a willingness to reward those whose contributions have been significant.

However, a number of organizations, in the government and semi-government sector, stick to the age-old time-tested 'promotion by seniority'. This is not to ruffle feathers but meritocracy takes the backseat with such a policy. There is a breath of fresh air likely to blow in the government sector too in the near future where bright employees could have some hope.

When job-hopping becomes the norm the usual promotion policy might not work to retain outstanding employees whose contribution could make a big difference to the fortunes of an organization. It might appear strange that mere financial inducement is not enough to woo and retain good employees. However, it is estimated that about 66.3 per cent Indian companies have a reward strategy for superior performance, not necessarily by promoting someone. That could prove to be a powerful motivator for others to work harder and get the coveted reward bonus. They look to a management policy that encourages talent, nurtures it and gives it opportunities to grown within or outside. Thus 'marketability' of an employee could be the yardstick for an employee to stick to a job. In fact, certain enlightened managements make it a point to see that their employees are 'marketable' in the job market so that they could find an outside place to work, if they so wish or if there is a downturn in their business, which could mean layoffs and retrenchment.

An employee is always looking for challenges. He loves to accept challenges willingly. That's the excitement, which pumps the adrenaline in an individual. A promotion could be just that force which drives a person to achieve excellence. No one wants to fail even without trying. The management should create the right environment where achievers are recognized and rewarded. That need not be limited to those who have met with success. The ingenuity is to recognize even those who tried hard but couldn't succeed due to various factors, internal and external. *Thus risk-takers too should get their just rewards and recognition*. Such an act will send out a strong message that a management recognizes those who tried hard despite heavy odds but didn't succeed which was not held out against them for not promoting. Promotion could be a powerful incentive for those who wish to excel and show that they could scale greater heights if only a management gives them the right environment and incentives.

> Indian companies use a mix of fast-track career paths, global salaries, stock options, performance bonuses, music rooms and gyms to retain talent.

An employee has every reason to aspire for promotion if he/she does the following during a period of time as stated below:

- You are doing a good job and everyone agrees with that label.
- *Multi-task*: You are doing more than one job at any one time successfully.
- Your time management is well organized that leaves with you free time to do something more that satisfies you. You will never say, "I am too busy" despite multi-functional jobs on hand.
- You are continuously upgrading your education and skills on your own initiative without even asking for anything like change in shift or financial assistance.
- You are constantly exploring the possibilities of growth within the organization by being proactive to look around for opportunities. If this does not work for long, then you might decide to quit for better prospects elsewhere.
- You do not rave and rant when you miss the bus of promotion time and again. You are dignified and would discuss with your superior calmly and constructively. May be there is something you have to improve to get that promotion. That is more galling when

your colleagues who started together have moved up leaving you behind. That is the right time to introspect and take an important decision in your career.

- If the boss praises you work often, that means he/she is satisfied with your work and attitude. That is the right time to hint that you are waiting for your promotion. Sometimes, there might not be any vacancy in your department and so you have to suggest where you could be fitted for the sake of your promotion that is due. Whether one likes it or not, one has to 'sell' oneself as the boss has too many other issues and cannot be expected to take care of your career all the time. That could be a formal or informal meeting with all the facts up your sleeve. You could be persuasive but not boastful or threatening, "Either promote me or I will quit." No boss likes such a blackmail threat to get one's promotion. *An employee is always on the lower rung of the power scale as the boss holds unlimited powers, which could be used against the assistant*. The higher-ups, in general, go by what the immediate boss has to say and would like to keep the pecking order in tact.

CHALLENGES

A few companies claim, "We give better opportunities to our people. Compensation alone does not work to keep the people." That is also true of promotions. Even a high-flyer, after a while, he wants more from life than power, position, money and perks. That is what a company should be looking forward to see an individual's aspirations in life are reasonably fulfilled while working for a company. *There is more to life than work, work, work, and monetary and other compensations.*

Keeping up an employee's interest in the organization after a while is not easy. That person is looking for challenges and the management has to provide such opportunities for the individual to learn and gain experience. For instance, designating a manager to look after a project as a team leader would expose that person to all sorts of challenges, internal and external as well. The manager is excited and a bit apprehensive too on the outcome of the project of which he is the sole leader. Of course, there are higher-ups who too could be consulted. But the challenge is for that manager do almost everything himself but taking the members of the team along. He would like to involve the boss only when needed and to keep that person appraised of the progress.

A manager has a lot to learn when a project or a task is handed over to that person to be executed independently. All the experience he has gained could prove useful in carrying out the project work to a successful conclusion. That is the real challenge managers look for. Job satisfaction is one aspect of a job. The other is the challenge at the workplace, which brings out the best in each individual. *When a person is concentrating on the challenge on hand, he/she does not think about promotion or any other incentive.*

A few challenges that could be given to a manager/supervisor/ employee are detailed in the Table below:

TABLE

- A new job
- Additional (multi) tasks
- Project work
- Team leader
- Training others
- Overseas assignment
- Further study/overseas seminar/workshop
- Sabbatical (leave of absence with full pay) that allows a person free time to do anything he/she likes for a period of one to two years on company's payroll.

The above list is by no means complete or exhaustive. Sometimes it is possible the employee is sent to do volunteer work, in time of distress like natural disaster—floods, droughts, earthquake, and tsunami. These might soften the blow of not getting a promotion when it is due to that person. However, the crave for promotion is so universal and tremendous that time and again the individual feels he/she has been let down by the management. *No sops could assuage that hurt feeling of an individual who justifiably thinks he/she deserved to be promoted, the sooner, the better*. Perhaps, some of the measures suggested could help to get over the feeling of dejection by the person affected, for instance when the employee is asked to take up an overseas assignment.

CASE STUDY

Gopal was a first level management officer (M1) in a MNC who had joined the company when he was rather 'old' at the age of 32 years. However, he had already put in about 9 years experience in R & D of a large public sector unit that assured him a higher starting salary in the new assignment. There was the usual adjustment problem whenever a new person joins another company. It took a while for Gopal to establish himself and was confirmed as a management officer after the mandatory six months probation period. He was put in charge of one of the sections in the quality control department.

Once during the annual increment meeting with the factory manager, Gopal opened his heart and wanted to know why he had to stay stagnant in the M1 cadre despite his background of many years of experience in a reputed company earlier. "Sir, I would appreciate if the management takes care of its people rather than I go on pleading my own case every year," Gopal's remarks stunned the factory manager who was tongue-tied. However, the departmental head Soni remarked, "Sir, let him say what he wants." It took a while to convince the management that Gopal deserved a promotion, as his work was impressive.

The only problem was promotions were limited in any year and that too each unit had its priority and 'quota.' As a result, Gopal was denied his due promotion for a number of years. It took him more than five years to be promoted to the second higher management level (M2). Fortunately the story had a happy ending. The management in all its wisdom felt that the present position Gopal was holding too needed upgrading and so the next promotion list had Gopal's name, to everyone's satisfaction. When the factory manager announced the promotion Gopal was stoic. "Are you not happy?" the factory manager wanted to know. Gopal just smiled and said "Thank you." In fact a few emotions went through his mind. "Better late than never," he consoled himself. "Does the factory manager expects me to dance a jig on hearing the announcement? After all 'promotion delayed is promotion denied.' Any way why should I explain all this now? This is not the occasion. However, let me be civil enough to accept the promotion gracefully and thank the management."

HOW TO HANDLE DISGRUNTLED EMPLOYEES

It is an undeniable fact that promotion causes heartburns in many than joy and thrill in a few selected persons. Those who are lucky or deserving a promotion, would be happy that at last the organization has recognized their contribution. For the majority it is a sad day and a day where their hopes and expectations are dashed to the ground by what they think is management's faulty promotional policy. "How could the management promote my colleague Mr. Roy and leave me out? I am senior, better qualified, and my contribution, I think is far more significant than Mr. Roy," moans a colleague of Mr. Roy who is disappointed the management overlooked his case for promotion once again. How to assuage the hurt feelings of many is an issue that needs to be tackled by the management sincerely and sensitively. "We have the right to decide promotions. If some people are not happy, it's their problem. We cannot please everyone, you know," would be the comment of a senior executive who is on the team to whet promotions. No doubt that executive is right but one should not forget the people have egos and emotions. If they feel sad and disappointed they would show it in many ways. Some mature persons keep their feelings to themselves stoically and carry on their routine as before. A few react violently and abuse their bosses. There is another category that is difficult to deal with as they sulk and show less enthusiasm in their work than before but they take care that the boss does not catch them on the wrong foot.

As stated earlier, promotion should be selective if it should serve as a motivational tool. *Not everyone every time could be promoted as the meaning of promotion would lose all its meaning*. Obviously, only a few are happy and overjoyed while the majority is unhappy. In fact, some of the employees, who were in the line of promotion, would be the ones who would really feel that the management has not been fair to them. A few others take all these in their stride, "If I don't get a promotion that's bad but that's not the end of the world." For some it could be a case of 'grapes are sour' while others it's disappointment coupled with jealousy. "How could my colleague get promoted while I have been left behind?" is an often-asked question. A few others are more realistic, "I didn't deserve a promotion and I didn't expect it either. So why should I be disappointed?" could be the remark of a pragmatic person who has taken disappointment, if any, in his/her stride. Often the boss would have told his/her assistants during formal and informal contacts that the chance of promotion was practically nil due to various factors. In such a case the degree of disappointment, being forewarned, would be much less.

COUNSELLING

Counselling a person who has just missed the promotion bus is not easy but needs patience, sympathy and understanding. His/her feelings of hurt and disappointment cannot be wished away easily. That person knows there are many hurdles to be crossed before a person gets promoted. He/she wants the boss to do all that would be necessary to get him/her promoted. When a person, who is not promoted, is wallowing in self pity, the least the boss could do is to sympathize with him/her and explain how he/she tried his/her best to put up the case with the higher ups. Sometimes such free and frank talk helps to apply the healing touch. However, if that person is disappointed despite the fact that his/her performance was below standard, the boss should not give any false promises but tell that person politely but firmly that the performance should improve drastically before his/her case could be considered for promotion. People should not be under any delusion if they think they have done a great job, which is not supported by the boss's independent assessment.

Some of the trauma of missing a promotion could be taken care of if there is regular interaction between the assistant(s) and the boss, not limited to the once in six/twelve monthly performance appraisals. *There should be a better understanding between the two when each could talk freely and frankly discussing the issue of promotion under a given set of circumstances.* Obviously, the boss should be open to tell the assistant what he/she thinks about his/her work and the possibility of climbing up the ladder in the near future. No promises should be made that could be used against the boss later on. *Caution is the word while discussing the promotion issue with the assistant.* However, a vague promise does not help the assistant either.

Employees are often not aware of the various steps that are taken in an organization for deciding promotion of employees. A shroud of secrecy and mystery surrounds such an exercise, which need not be so. People should become knowledgeable about the various stages how a promotion case is decided. A management has to make its promotion policy loud and clear. It has to be merit-based and more importantly, seen to be fair by the majority of the employees. An idea, which is finding favour, is to have an internal committee to whet the cases for promotion before they are put up to the next higher level. Each department head is present during such a "promotion whetting meeting" that gives an opportunity for everyone present to discuss the promotion cases in an unbiased manner. There are always likes and dislikes about some of the candidates put up for promotion that cannot be helped. Each departmental head that puts up his/her candidate has to argue in favour of his/her proposal. Other departmental heads might also give their comments, which could be favourable or critical. Only when a consensus is reached, the accepted list of names are sent up to the next higher level. The proceedings of such a meeting are kept confidential. Obviously, there is some 'sieving' done and only a few selected cases, agreed to by consensus, would be put up for approval to the next higher level of management.

That is a fair assessment by not only the immediate boss but also the peers too in the presence of the factory/general manager. It might appear strange that a prospective candidate for promotion has to make a good impression upon not only his/her immediate boss and the higher boss but other departmental heads which that person might be interacting from time to time. That is a positive factor in carrying a promotion proposal through. However, hurdles could be created if some departmental head/senior manager objects to a person's promotion. It is not uncommon for a boss to state helplessly to his/her assistant confidentially, "What can I do? So and so is not in favour of your promotion." What impressions senior managers carry about a person is important through that person's conduct, dedication, work output, dignified behaviour, ability to interact with others and communication skills. *This is not to suggest that one should actively lobby to get a promotion by influencing other senior managers besides your own boss*. A point is made that it would help the case if that person has already made a good impression on senior managers/departmental heads who matter too in the decision-making through good work, communication skill and conduct.

Here is a typical example of the process of whetting cases put up for promotion:

> Employee's work highly satisfactory→Boss recommends for promotion→Departmental head concurs, with his/her recommendation→Review by peers and recommend consensus candidates for promotion→Factory/General Manager signs the recommendation list with his/her comments→Board of directors takes final decision→Promotion paper sent by HRD to the person via proper channels.

DEVIOUS WAYS

There are complaints and innuendoes that a few employees undertake all sort of devious means to get promoted. Some of these are exaggerated no doubt, who doesn't love gossips and juicy stories, while there could be some truth in the allegations. For example, being pleasant to the boss is not a crime but if someone becomes a 'yes' man, then this is a sure sign that person is not true to his/her own self and is trying to curry favour from the boss for being on 'his/her' side all the time. Running errands for the boss is another contentious issue. If the boss or his family member is not well and is in the hospital it would be the right thing to offer help. However, if any one deviates from professional ethics in trying to overdo to please the boss that person loses his/her individuality and becomes identified with the boss who is always powerful and who could dish out favours and goodies. Such persons are sarcastically labelled the 'lapdog' of the boss. Colleagues would be wary of cultivating friendship with such persons who could carry tales to the boss to the detriment of their own interests.

Visiting the boss's family, with your spouse and children, is socializing and cannot be faulted. However, if this becomes frequent, tongues would wag, especially if the boss accepts gifts from the assistant. *Being on the right side of your boss is a good idea*. That does not mean you concur with whatever the boss says all the time. After all, you have your ego, professionalism as well as personality, which are important too.

> Maintaining correct relationship with the boss is an art and one has to practice it depending upon the nature of the boss.

Some of the bosses welcome guests while others frown upon if you intrude on his/her privacy. Talking shop is not the done thing, as this could be done in the office. Currying favour with the boss is degrading oneself. There are horror stories where the boss asks the assistant to carry out certain illegal work with a promise that he/she would be rewarded handsomely. That very thought that you are being used to further the interest of the boss through dangerous and illegal ways should warn you and even at the cost of your job, you must say a firm "NO" to such illegal and unethical dealings. That would show strength of character of the assistant if he/she stands up to the boss and tells him, "Enough, is enough, Sir." Unfortunately in a few cases the assistant is victimized for being right and ethical but that cannot be helped if one is true to one's own conscience.

WHISTLE-BLOWERS

We have glorious and stirring reports of individuals who are known as "Whistle-blowers" who risk everything to expose illegal, hazardous and unethical activities of not only their bosses but even of the CEOs, if they are involved in any cover-up to hoodwink the gullible. *Every business needs such ethical and brave persons so that they could warn the regulators and higher-ups that something fishy was going on*. They are not afraid of victimization or even dismissal in their single-minded mission to do everything right in the public interest. However, one has to be careful and gather all the relevant facts before alerting the higher-ups or going public with the sensational disclosure. He/she cannot act on mere suspicion but on hard facts supported by authentic documents and data that could be proved in a court of law. There is no place for sensationalizing for the sake of publicity, as such premature unsubstantiated expose would nullify all the good work done and damage one's own credibility.

It also means the internal auditors and external auditors would have to be independent and swear by the truth and nothing but the truth. They should not become mere pawns in the hands of senior managers/directors and the CEOs because they are the eyes and ears of the management. Timely warning of underhand dealings, frauds, tax evasion and other unethical practices should be brought to the notice of the CEO and the Chairman of the Board of Directors. And lastly, if such warnings are not heeded by the top men within the organization, the person who is charged up and who wants to play an upright game should become a 'whistle-blower' risking his/her job but that person would have the moral satisfaction of listening to his/her own conscience for the public good. *Public has a short memory for good things but a long memory for anything bad.* So it would take a long time and sincere efforts to get back into the good books of the public once a company has been caught red-handed doing illegal and unethical practices and business. People excuse a company for making a loss but never if it indulges in illegal and unethical activities that harm its credibility, cheat the government and the public as well.

6

How to Manage Attrition

—Take it in your stride

Much has been talked about the need to control attrition in any organization, especially the fast growing BPO industry where this is upwards of 20 per cent. Management would like to train young employees, and would do their best to retain them at least for five years if not more. However, for the youngsters 'the lawn next door is greener' than what they have. Job-hopping, whether one likes it or accepts it or not, is a fact of life. The question is how best to retain employees who would be loyal to the organization and would like to grow with it. That is easier said than done given the complex issues involved. *Loyalty to an organization is not a commodity that could be bought in the marketplace for a price.* That could come through by various proactive actions of the organization that hopes to retain employees for a longer period. For a new employee the first few days/weeks/months are critical for his/her very survival in an alien environment. The ease by which that new employee could adjust to it could have a lasting effect.

> There is a school of thought that states attrition is not a bad thing after all.

That might sound strange for both the employer as well as the employee. How can attrition could be good is a question that is often asked. Attrition brings in certain changes—in the employer and the employee. For the employer at first sight, attrition means more work and more investment in new greenhorn employees. The investment made in the form of training, motivation and other charges would go waste for the employer. Moreover, it has more work to be done—recruitment, training, motivation, equipment costs and so on. That might not be much but nevertheless costs do occur that are non-productive and that is wasteful expenditure anyway. The silver lining for the organization is it gives an opportunity for it to introspect. It can rethink whether its salary structure needs to be competitive or certain changes in the organization are needed that would attract and retain young talent. That might also make the organization replan its human side of the enterprise to make it more employee-friendly. That is the reason why a detailed exit interview with the employee who has decided to quit would help in getting the feedback that would lead to changes, which finally would prove useful to the enterprise.

An employee who quits too is uncertain of the future. That person had quit the organization with the hope and expectation of something better. It is also possible that the employee quit for matters other than finance or compensation package. Perhaps that employee found the organization too stifling for his/her creative work due to its policies. The boss could have been nasty causing heartburns all the time. Or the working hours, especially those BPO employees who operate in the graveyard shift, find it too tough to cope with. There are many reasons why an employee quits an organization seeking better fortune or work environment elsewhere. Hence it's impossible to satisfy the ambition of everyone who wants to climb the hierarchical ladder faster than anyone else or provide the ideal workplace environment that would satisfy the fastidious. Nevertheless, the management has to introspect deeply if there is large-scale desertion from the company.

That does not mean, however, the management sits with folded hands and allows people to leave without any proactive approach. It has to find out why the attrition is taking place in the first place. If it is a question of lower salary/wages/perks as compared to the industry average, then it is time for the management do something positive about it. It is also possible the work environment needs to be improved so that employees work in a quiet and peaceful environment devoid of tension and anxiety, to the extent it can by improving the infrastructure—air-conditioning, indoor plants, pleasing décor, ergonomic tables and chairs, a nice carpet, appropriate lighting, art pieces on the wall, light unobtrusive music, open sitting but with a few cabins without doors, recreation room with radio/TV/music system, gym, meditation room, library, coffee/tea dispensing machines and so on. Free transport to and from the workplace is another issue that is important to a new employee, especially women.

> Salary and perks do attract youngsters but the fascination for these would soon go away after the initial enthusiasm.

A few problems faced by the BPO staff are detailed in the Table on the next page.

TABLE

- Average employee tenure of 1.5 years; less in domestic companies
- Only one in four believe that the present job advances his/her career
- At 54 working hours per week, industry endorses a long-hours culture
- 75 per cent employee joined the Labour Union to improve pay and working conditions
- Employee security, long work hours are major concerns

What an employee desires is that he/she is given due respect for his/her contribution to the well being of the organization. That person does not want to be treated as a mere cog in the production or process chain. Another important aspect is the workplace environment should be conducive for a person to work peacefully and have freedom to give vent to his/her imagination, which could bring out innovative ideas. Treating an employee as a human being is another vital aspect how an employee would vibe with an organization that cares for him/her. Hence each manager (boss) should develop interpersonal skills that help in caring for the people under that person's control.

A manager should be a philosopher, friend, guide and coach that every employee under him/her looks upon as a person to be trusted.

WHEN YOUR FAVOURITE EMPLOYEE QUITS

A manager pins hope that his able assistant would take over one day, so that he is in a position to take up a higher responsibility. To declare oneself 'surplus' should be the aim of all managers who do not see their assistants as threats but as opportunities for their own advancement. After grooming an assistant, it is but natural that he is expected to step into your shoes. Thus, he would get all the help, guidance and encouragement needed to groom him. He is your blue-eyed boy waiting in the wings to take over from you. Ideally, career development of each employee should be planned properly and not on *ad hoc* basis.

The day the assistant comes to you with his resignation letter could well be the bad and unlucky day for the manager who had pinned so much of hope in the boy. It is but natural that he stares at the paper and the person in front repeatedly just to make sure it is not a bad dream but a reality he has to come to grips with. Short of breast-beating the manager is downcast and won't say anything but to mutter that 'he would look into it.' After the assistant leaves the office, he has a look again at the resignation letter just to make sure he has read it properly. He doesn't disclose this information to anyone, not even his own boss at least that day. He wants time to think deeply and also wants his assistant to sleep over it.

Next day, the manager is on tenterhooks waiting for his assistant to drop in and, hopefully, asking for the resignation letter back. As the day wears on, he is disappointed that his assistant hasn't changed his mind overnight. Slowly, the enormity of the situation sinks in. He is left with no choice but to call his assistant to his office for a heart-to-heart chat. He doesn't find fault with the assistant on whom he showers his praises and tells him, unabashedly, what an asset he has been to the team. "Why don't you give a second thought to your resignation? Why don't you change your mind?" He holds vaguely the carrot of awards/rewards he could hope to receive if he withdrew his resignation. "I can put in a word to my boss and, hopefully, something good would come out," he promises. The assistant, sometimes, falls for such an inducement, and might agree to withdraw the resignation. That would be a happy ending for what could have been a sad episode.

If the assistant insists that his resignation should be accepted, the manager too might act tough. If inadvertently the boss has come to know to which organization the assistant is heading, then he might even blackmail him. "You know, there is a policy (may be true or not!) that the company you are joining might not take you if we request that management. So you will be having no job in the end," which could be just a bluff. *The manager in an attempt to confuse his assistant might paint a dark picture of the new company he is likely to join.* Such a strategy is not ethical but what can anyone do if the boss tries all sorts of dubious means to retain a valuable employee. Then he might launch into a praise of the present organization he is working. "Ours is a progressive company. Those who work hard and are loyal would be rewarded. So the choice is yours." By subtle hints the boss tries to brainwash the assistant to stay back.

The assistant who is firm in his determination to seek greener pasture is not cowed down or taken by such glib talk. He might politely tell his boss, "Sir, thank you for your good advice and suggestions. I appreciate these but I have made up my mind to resign. So please let us part as friends", might clinch the matter, as far the immediate boss is concerned. But that's only half the battle won. The boss has a boss too and that could prove to be the real hurdle. The moment the boss approaches his boss regarding the assistant's letter of resignation there could be some heart searching and mutual bickering.

"How come you didn't me tell me about it earlier?" the senior manager could react, as if that mattered. He might suggest, "Let us offer him a promotion/additional responsibility/overseas training." If such a carrot doesn't appeal to the person who wants to quit, the only course left for the management is to accept the resignation with regret but with no hard feelings. That's the time for the departmental head to inform his people that one of the employees is quitting for better prospects and the management has wished him good luck. That would leave a better impression on the people than trying to keep the resignation of any assistant under the wraps for long giving a chance for the rumour mills to work overtime while putting the management in poor light. *No one is indispensable and an organization has to learn to live with such a reality*. In fact, it should make parting of ways smoother and dignified with no bitterness and hard feelings. That could be a plus point for the organization as the word-of-mouth publicity would show that organization in good light and as a humane company while dealing with people.

> Resignation of an employee, however valuable he/she might be, is part of the attrition process in an organization.

Some degree of turnover is inevitable and, according to experts, necessary. That would give an opportunity for that employee and for the organization to find their true market-worth. A bright employee could leave a void for some time, until a new employee is recruited and trained. However, if the turnover is excessive, it is time for the management to sit up and take note. It might have to change its recruitment/compensation policies to attract and retain good people. A note of warning: Don't take any hasty decision favouring an employee when he threatens to quit.

CASE STUDY

Goel was a good assistant in an R & D set-up in a big company. He used to visit his customers to get an idea about present and future needs of valued customers so that the company's design could reflect on customers' preferences. His work was good and he was recommended for a brief overseas training. His design concepts and vision improved much further after that orientation programme and his work began to impress the department head. However, promotion eluded Goel who was pining for a promotion though he had got hefty raises in his salary from year to year. During one of his visits to his customers, Goel talked freely about his promotion or lack of it. The director of the company remarked seriously, "Why don't you join us? We could offer you double the present salary and perks and designate you as assistant departmental head." That was sweet music to the ears of Goel who told the director he would consider the offer and revert soon.

Goel lost no time in meeting his departmental head and talked to him about his promotion, which according to him was overdue. "Sir, I am sorry to state that I might take up the offer from another company which has offered me a big raise and an attractive position in their R & D department. I will have to decide it soon." That was a bombshell to the department head who rushed to meet his boss, the factory manager. "Oh, is that so? It's a pity. I don't want Goel to leave us as he is too valuable, you know. However, don't promise him anything right now, as I have to discuss his promotion case with the Head Office. Please ask him to wait for another week."

The Director Personnel was the lone voice on the Board of Management, who objected to this out-of-turn and out-of-schedule promotion. "What would be our credibility if we promote him? Don't you think that would set a bad precedence?" was the argument of the Director. But he was overruled. "We have to retain Goel, come what may. He is too valuable to be lost to another competitor," the CEO opined and his decision was final. The promotion paper was typed post-haste and signed in record time. Goel was pleasantly surprised that he was at the receiving end of a promotion paper within three days of talking to his boss about his promotion. He was beaming with joy as he came out of the Factory Manager's cabin. His colleagues were not too happy about that sudden surprising development but as a matter of courtesy congratulated him on his elevation.

Who can stop tongues wagging? The news spread like wildfire not only within the organization but also even outside. The management became a laughing stock. "Let us call this a new tool of 'motivation' – promotion by blackmail!" stated one senior manager who had to answer his people why they too were not considered for out-of-turn promotions. After setting up such a bad precedence, the management had a hard time assuaging the hurt feelings of many senior employees who had worked sincerely and loyally without any recognition. "Should I also wave a letter of appointment from another company before I am considered invaluable and so deserved a promotion?" was the cynical remarks of a few disgruntled employees. It took a long time before restoring the credibility of the management. By pleasing and placating one employee, the management had upset many loyal employees who too deserved recognition.

Moral: Do not bend backwards to please a person who has made up his/her mind to seek greener pastures elsewhere.

How to engage your employees to reduce attrition is an important aspect of working in an organization. A few tips are presented in the Table below:

TABLE

- Engage its talented workforce and involve them in a long-term relationship within the company to fight the high attrition rates they are faced with
- Create culture of recognition throughout the organization that appreciates excellence, which in turn drives performance in the organization
- Salary no longer the main constituent of satisfied staff or will ensure their retention
- Recognition, timely awards, conducive climate that provides

motivation for the employees to perform consistently in the pursuit of career ambitions

- Lasting relationship, workplace conducive atmosphere and motivational values more important than money
- Relationship is a function of interactions
- Organizations must make people wanted and appreciated
- Set clear goals for each and every employee
- Be serious about recognizing people's achievements
- Support employees' career development through innovative measures
- Initiate leadership development programmes for employees
- HR is no longer human resources but human relations
- Emotional engagement and human bonding with employees is important

The under-mentioned paragraph contains a new mantra to retain employees:

- Provide employees with a comfortable and interactive atmosphere.
- Give avenues to relieve the stress from routine work.
- A corporate fitness centre could boost productivity at the workplace, improved job satisfaction and a healthy workforce.
- Engage in stress-buster activities such as get-togethers, adventure trips, employee musical bands/singing groups, in-house interactive newsletters, annual picnics, sports events, variety entertainment, quiz/music competitions, setting up of holiday homes in exciting locales.
- Give a platform for employees to voice their opinions about the workplace and give their suggestions.
- Employees must feel, "This is my dream company where I want to work for long."
- In-house newsletters contain information about birthday parties, employees' achievements, readers' suggestions, comments, and criticisms.
- Encourage employees to do what they want.
- Some companies organize monthly one-day cultural events and competitions.
- Encourage employees to dine together for which an allowance is given.
- Give the employees a sense of being looked after by positive work
- On public holidays and festival occasions, festivities are held within the office premises to make employees feel at home.
- Organize occasional get-togethers and quarterly events scheduled to improve the bonding between the employees.
- Involve the employees' families at least in a few activities of the company like cultural/sports events.

- Take interest in the employee's family too by providing job opportunities for the spouses, may be part-time, and give educational assistance to their children such as merit-*cum*-means scholarships. Offer educational loans at low interest to make the employee feel that the company is looking after not only himself/herself but the family too.

The three main reasons why an employee quits a job are:

- Find better pay elsewhere
- Better career development
- Personal reasons

The Table below shows a few more tips to reduce attrition and retain talent:

TABLE

5 ways to retain talent:
• Sign-on bonus • Retention bonus • Stock options • Skill-based bonuses • Overseas assignments
Source : *India Today* (February 5, 2008).

Dealing with Women Employees

- India's booming IT and IT-enabled service industries are a favourite destination of job-seeking women, which is at present 30 percent but likely to rise to 45 per cent by 2010.
- This is due to the inclusive human resources policies of the Indian software firms, which recruit, train, retain and promote women employees as a strategic business plan.
- Empower women employees and create conducive environment to grow equally at the workplace. Improve scope for professional advancement.
- Inadequate representation of women at top levels of management
- Plan to have flex-working hours for women who could devote adequate time to their office as well as home.

Problems of over-work and stress at workplace, including BPO jobs:

- Mental fatigue
- Depression

- To be or not to be feeling
- Lack of communication
- Poor health
- Signs of listlessness results in increased job hopping and rising intra-national migration

A few tips to beat the burnout are given in Table below:

TABLE

- Spread the workload and responsibility
- Do not accept work that is not in your field
- Make the workplace a pleasant environment
- If possible take a shot nap during break
- Avoid too much of caffeine
- Exercise regularly
- Eat well and regularly. Avoid junk food
- Keep your sense of humor

— *Business Today Tips*

Here are a few tips on how to meet challenges of HR:

- Shortage of qualified persons due to too many projects.
- Shortage of talented persons who are exposed to international standards.
- Certain sectors neglected while there is an over-supply of qualified people.
- Retaining talent is always a challenge—encourage learning to be become more 'marketable'.
- Managing expectations of employees.
- Inculcating values in employees.
- Develop second-rung leaders.
- *Managing employees with a diverse background, educational qualification, experience and culture.*

Case Study

A Multi National Company (MNC) based in Mumbai had a problem of getting good candidates and retaining them for their Management Graduate Apprentice (GA) scheme. After one year of training, the GAs would be absorbed into the management cadre. The company found that campus interview was one of the major sources of GAs but had failed to attract the better talents. The Director, HRD, suggested that the GAs should be given a higher starting salary to begin with and the training programme itself should be revamped to make it interesting and challenging. The change in the training schedule meant that the last four months of their training the GAs would be placed in the department where they would be finally posted. However, it was stipulated that the GAs should have a choice of the department where they would like to work, to the extent that was possible. The training manager, in charge of the GAs was requested to guide them individually and see that their interest was kept up throughout the training. These changes made a difference to the attitude of the GAs that helped to retain most of the graduates, though some left for higher studies or other companies. The company policy was revised to make the stipend offered to the GAs more attractive in keeping with the competition in any particular region.

Job-hopping

Before liberalization and globalization, the job opportunities were limited. Only a few Public Sector Units (PSUs) and a few big private companies existed which gave opportunities for employment. In fact an employee who resigned his/her job from one PSU was not allowed to seek employment in another PSU. Strangely, such a rule was applied by a few MNCs too in certain regions to prevent qualified and experienced persons from ditching one unit and join another one for better salary/perks and career advancement.

Job security and employee loyalty were taken for granted. In fact, a few employees used to put up on their houses stone plaques with their name and the company they were working for. A person would join a company at a young age and continue to work till that person retired. Sometimes an employee would be posted to another PSU set-up as a measure of de-centralization. The question of retrenchment did not arise. The PSUs were assumed to create employment opportunities to the people, with or without being profitable. That was because the Centre took care to bail out a company in the red, as it did not want to take the unpopular measure of closing a loss-making unit for fear of popular resentment, unrest by employees and agitation by labour union(s).

However, with the growth in the industrial sector, with more MNCs setting up shop and the phenomenal growth of the service sector (which is now about 60% of the GDP, with 40% GDP in the manufacturing sector), job opportunities have been created everywhere—BPO industry, IT-related services, Internet-related business, hospitality industry, health-care, health clubs, gyms, mobile service provider, organizations dealing with environmental concerns, NGOs and the list is ever growing. Salary/wages/perks are at a record high, unthinkable in the past with new entrants in most industry drawing over Rs. 5000 per month at the entry level. The Sixth Pay Commission (2008) has offered a big salary hike for Central Government employees across the board.

The above has created a situation where a person, especially the one who wants to grow fast, has a good opportunity to shop for better jobs all the time. He/she never thinks of the loyalty factor when the only reason to change is to improve one's own earnings and better career prospects. *Job opportunities especially for the bright talented youngster have never been so good.*

However, "a rolling stone gathers no moss," is also true. The reason why a bright student would like to work for a year or two before taking up higher studies is an indication that hands-on work experience is valuable and better than any theoretical lesson from a classroom.

> How can a 'high-flyer' be retained in an organization is a question that is a matter of discussion at the highest level in any management.

Obviously, the management is aware of the contribution of such persons who could make a big difference. The fact that some companies are offering the 'sky' to a fresh IIM/IIT graduate is an indication how a talented person is being wooed with the expectation that he/she would be a big contributor to the future of the company. However, the management is aware that such a person is ambitious and expects to rise faster and so needs special attention to retain such a person. It is also possible that the high-flyer is not as promising as presumed at the time of recruitment. In such case, the management reluctantly takes a view that person has to leave the organization, as it cannot retain someone who is not worth all the investment.

Some managements feel the efforts to woo the brightest talent is not worth the money. They know that such a person might not stick with the company for long due to various reasons, including a competitive offer, disillusionment with the company, and finding the work not to his/her liking and other personal reasons like wanting to go abroad or take up higher studies. What such a management does is to target not the top-most talent but the above average talent with the expectation that such persons are not too ambitious and so likely to stick with the organization for some years at least, though they could be proved wrong.

> In the rush to garner top talent, by offering astronomical salaries, problems are created within the organization.

Whether the management likes it or not, tongues begin to wag pointing out that the so-called top-talented person is not so bright or useful after all. That could be plain jealousy or that person meets with cold response from the existing staff that makes working together difficult. The psychological effect of hiring some one by paying a huge salary could be counter-productive in the long-run considering the fact that those loyal to the company feel shortchanged and their salary remains very much below that of a newcomer however bright he/she might be. That is an aspect that needs to be considered carefully by a management, which is headhunting for top talent, in our business milieu. It is rare that a new comer is welcomed with open arms until he/she proves to be a nice person and a good team player. Employees judge a newcomer to find out how he/she gets on with the existing employees, before he/she is accepted wholeheartedly as one of their own members of the team. The newcomer on his/her part should realize there is a certain invisible barrier to be breached before establishing sound working relations with the employees. *If he/she is modest and mixes freely with the employees, that person would have already won half the battle of minds towards establishing good relations.* It is indeed a trying period for a new comer to settle down and be accepted as a team player. During that 'trial' period, the newcomer would do well to listen more and talk less about his qualification and experience and be willing to learn from the people.

Wild Ducks

A few employees do not fit the description of a 'normal' person. He/she is exuberant and wants to do things in a manner thought fit by him/her. Unconventional behaviour and work are the norms for such persons who want to be labelled as 'wild ducks', which want to be free to fly. Dealing with such employees is not easy but they could turn out to be great innovators if nurtured properly by pandering to their whims and fancies, to the extent a management could tolerate. Such 'wild ducks' exist in each and every organization if only a management looks around carefully. Often such a person is a poor team player but a sound solo player that makes difficult for a manager to put such a person in a team of likeminded employees. It is best they are given independent work like faultfinding, repair, audit, R&D where it is generally an individual work that matters with little interaction with others. Such 'wild ducks' have their own place in an organization and need not be sacked just because they are eccentric or poor team players.

The emphasis on youth makes life difficult for older employees who have been loyal and working for a long time in an organization contributing their mite. When they see a youngster half of their age, being recruited at more than their salary, they are naturally upset. They might sulk and not extend cooperation to the newcomer. However, the mature old timer would accept such a situation stoically and render all assistance to the newcomer to settle down. That is where a manager has to watch the situation carefully and guide the newcomer as well as the existing employees that change was inevitable and one has to accept a given situation with grace.

Attrition in an organization is a cause of concern. It disrupts normal work as an employee leaves the organization creating avoid for some time at least. "No one is indispensable," the management might state, putting on a brave face. But it also knows, work suffers a while and it has to start looking for a replacement soon, which could be a long drawn out procedure. However, the bright side of attrition is sometimes a troublesome person leaves an organization and everyone heaves a sigh of relief. But if a good person quits the organization most of his/her colleagues feel sorry for that person. The blame game could start with the employees holding the management directly responsible for the unfortunate exit of that person.

An employee thinks twice before quitting a good organization. The 'pasture on the other side of the fence' could be greener. But there is uncertainty while a person opts out of an established organization for a not-so-sound company, just because he/she got an offer of higher salary/perks. There is a genuine fear of change from comfort and safety into an uncertain unknown zone. *For some others, "boss trouble" is the determining factor*. They are so fed up with the attitude of their boss that they would even quit in a huff and get away from a nagging boss who had made their life miserable. Others who too are not happy with their bosses wait for an opportunity to leave the organization. What is not so certain is the person who has adjustment problem with his/her boss could face a similar situation in another set up too. That could be a matter of 'from frying pan into the fire'. The topic of attrition is interesting and various organizations have dealt with that problem in diverse ways.

Regular assessment of employees is well established in organizations as the HRD has turned professional and expects each department head to spend time in assessing the employees under his/her control once in six months at least. That is a valuable tool if conducted in a free and fair manner. Often the latest impression of an employee is what the boss remembers and so the assessment is biased to that extent. All the good work done by an employee over the year turns useless if the boss has memory for a bad incident that happened only the previous week. Such subjectivity is a matter of concern but such biased assessment cannot be helped unless the boss's boss is in the know how of that particular employee's work record over the year.

Exit Interview

Some companies do conduct the exit interview in a fair and free manner while others do it cursorily or not at all. Such companies are missing a valuable input from an employee who might have served the company for long years. It is also true the employee might not be forthcoming as to why he/she has chosen to quit. There is always the fear that the management might be vindictive and harm that employee's interest in the company he/she is joining. Another tendency is to browbeat the employee and belittle his/her contribution. Such tactics are not ethical or professional and defeats the very purpose of an exit interview, which is supposed to get a feedback from the employee why he/she has quit and what are his/her suggestions and criticisms which could be used for corrective measures. A senior officer of the HRD could conduct the exit interview with an open mind.

The important points from the interview should be brought to the notice of the managers of all departments. However, a sensitive matter such as the employee's personal problem with his/her boss should not be circulated to others but only to the departmental head concerned. It could be interesting to find out if the attrition rate is more in a specific department. That could be either due to a particular departmental head is not responsive to his/her people's needs or there is a demand outside for specific expertise from a department like R & D which is beyond the control of the department head.

Exit interview is a valuable tool for getting a feedback from the employee who has put in the papers. That could spur positive and corrective measures in the organization.

What an employee thinks about an organization is important due to the 'word-of-mouth' publicity, whether good or bad. That applies to someone who has decided to quit. Parting of ways should be smooth and friendly so that that person carries a good opinion of the company which he/she has decided to leave for any reason. The last thing he/she wants is to be humiliated at the time of quitting which could leave a bitter taste and a poor opinion of the organization where that person worked for long. "Let us part as friends," should be the aim of both the employer and the employee.

7

Ushering in Change

—No change, no gain

Change is inevitable yet people are reluctant to change. For example, in the earlier days, when Banks introduced ATMs (Automatic Teller Machines), which are accessible 24 hours a day, people were not too keen to use these. However, customers gained confidence when they began to use these and found them very convenient. Thus any change be it technology, process, rules or procedure will have to be introduced gradually and in consultation with the users. Needless to state, these should be user-friendly. We cannot have change *per se*. It should serve some useful purpose. All intended changes will have to be put under the scanner just to make sure these are needed, user/environmentally friendly and improved quality of life. Mere cosmetic changes that use up scarce materials are a luxury we could live without.

> Successful change management is the true test of leadership quality since change is not only about the present but of the future too.

The fact is change is inevitable whether one likes it or accepts it or not. Those who wait for a while before accepting a change are disappointed that it won't go away by itself or wished away. For instance, banks have more or less changed over to electronic banking. In other words, the good old paper passbook is slowly but surely giving place to On-line access to one's bank account. Any time such information is available only to the user who has a secure password. By the click of the mouse the information could be printed out in a matter of seconds. *A few diehard conservative customers are wary about*

Internet banking. "What if someone breaks into my account and cleaned it up?" That is indeed a genuine fear, which cannot be dismissed, as there are stray cases where crooks have broken into the personal and confidential password codes of customers and used up all the money in customers' account. However, these isolated examples need not deter one from going in for Internet banking, taking all possible precautions to safeguard's password being secure and confidential. Nevertheless, a few conservative minded persons cling to the old way of life with a hope changes would pass over them. Unfortunately, such a hope is belied. The good news is the fact that the majority of the users want a change that makes their lives easier. Who does not want payment through the ECS system, which is automatic and hassle free? One does not have to stand in long lines for hours to pay a bill or get penalized if the due date of payment is over.

While credit/debit card is common in advanced countries, we in India are yet to go in on a large scale to such a convenient form of payment. 'Plastic money' has replaced 'paper money' in the advanced countries, barring exceptions. However, there are old-timers in the advanced countries too who would like to feel the crisp greenbacks or whatever currency they are so used to. They might have a credit/debit card but they prefer hard cash to plastic money which they cannot touch. The universal convenience of plastic money has reduced drastically the use of paper money. However, customers have to be on their guard as credit card/debit card fraud is a multi-million dollar 'business'. Sometimes the credit card companies are not so user-friendly. They are keen to sell their business but are not so cooperative enough to redress genuine problems faced by users. But by and large the use of credit/debit card is increasing at least in major towns and cities in our country. Yet shopping through credit/debit card is not so widespread as the shops, barring big stores and departmental stores, do not accept credit/debit card unlike in the advanced countries. However, all is not well with the ATMs—some times they refuse to work due to network problem, cash is out of the machine, card valid yet the machine states "it's invalid" and so on. *Nevertheless, for sheer convenience of a 24 hour banking, there is no substitute to an ATM*. We need more ATMs that could work through the intra-bank and inter-bank ATM networks. However, charges for use of 'other' bank ATMs should be reduced drastically to induce more customers to use the ATMs that save costs ultimately to the banks and at the same time provides a handy outlet for ready cash to customers without hassles. These issues are being addressed to by the Reserve Bank of India (RBI), which has issued guidelines to Banks with regard to problems faced by ATM users (2008).

CASE STUDY

> A change that's thrust upon the people concerned could produce negative reactions and ultimately could prove counter-productive.

Clocking in time of arrival/departure for workers in factories, and offices is common. However, an educational institution in the private sector in Bangalore decided to introduce punching in and punching out for the teachers, including the headmistresses. Discussions had taken place in the committee with most members agreeing to the proposal that involved purchase of a punching clock and a punching card for each teacher as well as non-teaching staff. That was done without consulting the teachers concerned as one fine day they were informed by the management committee that punching of cards to register their attendance would be introduced. It was mandated by the management committee that teachers should clock in at least 15 minutes prior to the daily assembly and the commencement of classes. A measure considered draconian by the affected teachers/other employees was the provision that if they were late by more than ten minutes on more than three occasions in a month, then they had to apply for a day's casual leave as compensation.

There was muted protest but no one dared to challenge the introduction, which was done ostensibly to improve 'attendance and discipline'. Perhaps the intention was good but in practice it suffered from the fact that the employees were not given a chance to give their opinion before making such a drastic change from the existing practice of signing the attendance register. The punching machine was introduced with much fanfare as a 'progressive' measure. But the teachers and other staff members were none too happy with the introduction of the time clock, which they thought was not only unnecessary but burdensome too. "If we have to lose a day's casual leave for being late more than three times, then why go to the school at all? We could as well stay back and enjoy our leave," was the reaction of the employees who resented the sudden introduction of a change in the system without prior discussion or their consent.

The employees were happiest when the time clock machine malfunctioned or it went out of order, which happened quite often. During such breakdowns, the register system was put back into service, much to the delight of the employees who hoped silently that the time clock would fail more often! The fall-out from the introduction of the punching machine was subtle. The teachers/non-teaching staff were not volunteering to stay back or work overtime. Any task designated by the management would be questioned and then only it was done reluctantly. Such a 'non-cooperation' attitude of the employees was noticed by a few members of the management committee who then began to wonder whether the change was really necessary and whether it was proving to be non-productive with the change in the attitude of the employees which was now definitely one of non-cooperation with the management.

Due to the dictatorial attitude of the management, the employees too thought that it would be right if they also stuck to the rules rather than go out of the way to be helpful and cooperate with the management.

Change is imperative, because without change a rot would set in. That is exactly what happened to ancient civilizations, corporations, leaders and even ordinary citizens. The only way to stay ahead of the game is to constantly change. They need tools and inspiration to change to meet future challenges. Instead of fighting a change, that could be in their own interests, people should accept any change, perceived to be useful, willingly and enthusiastically. There is no doubt a certain degree of inertia before one realizes the need for change. "Why should I accept that change? What's in it for me? Will it bring any benefit to meet me at all?" are some of the questions nagging someone faced with a change. Two-way communication would help in such a situation. *Often it is the fear of any change rather than the change itself that is holding back people from accepting the change voluntarily and without any pre-conceived notions*. How to make people accept a change without any problem is a matter of deep study and willingness on the part of the change-maker to be open and learn from experiences. Perforce that person(s) should be willing to listen to the objections/suggestions by those who are being targeted for change. Job rotation and multi-tasking were once considered against the interests of employees. However, the management could convince the employees it is for their good as it improved their chance of promotion inside the organization and their 'marketability' outside, if found inevitable. Involvement of the people concerned makes acceptance of a change easier as the people are convinced it's for their good.

> Marketing a change is a matter of skill and sincerity.

People do not appreciate *ad hoc* changes that are thrust upon them due to the whims of a CEO, manager, administrator, or political leadership. The change-seeker should assume there would be always some resistance to any change, as people do not accept a change quickly and that too voluntarily. There should be transparent honesty to listen and take action when people complain about changes that are hard to abide by. Any promise made to remedy a lacuna should be followed up sincerely. We should congratulate ourselves that in a vast country like ours, with low level of literacy, introduction of an Electronic Voting Machine (EVM) instead of a paper ballot and manual counting was possible due to the homework done by the people in the Election Commission. This dramatic change has saved paper and the results are out quickly instead of slow and laborious counting of paper ballots manually. In fact we are a step ahead of some of the advanced countries in this regard. Even the uneducated could easily understand and follow the routine for voting on the EVM. Initially, there were doubts the machines could be tampered with and results loaded in favour of any particular candidate. After a prolonged use, no such doubts exist now and EVMs are almost used exclusively throughout our vast nation.

> A slow and steady introduction of a change would be desirable, with a few exceptions.

For instance, though India adopted the metric system of weights and measurements long back, some of the advanced countries like the USA and the UK lag behind. Some of them still use the miles rather than kms, lbs instead of kgs though there is now a dual system in existence to familiarize the customers about the introduction of the metric system in the near future. However, another school of thought believes a change has to be sudden, immediate and irreversible to have the maximum impact. People would certainly grumble about such suddenness but in the larger interests such a move might be beneficial to the people at large in the short-term as well as long-term. For instance, if a Municipal Corporation of a city in India declares that spitting in public is punishable with a fine after one month of notification, there would be certainly some opposition to such a move. That happened in the case of compulsory introduction of helmets for all two-wheeler drivers and pinion riders in the interest of safety in case of an accident. The riders were unhappy that they had to invest in a helmet and some of them cared more for their appearance and comfort level rather than safety of their own heads. The policemen too were not too keen to enforce such a rule, which they thought was too draconian.

A change however good needs to be withdrawn or modified at least temporarily when it cannot be implemented without problems or it is facing a great deal of resistance and opposition from many people. For instance, some State governments introduced emission checks on vehicles. Unfortunately the consumers found that there were very few emission-check centers as a result there were great lines before such check stations. People complained about the high cost for check and sheer inconvenience caused to them. The government withdrew the order and made arrangements for more emission check stations to come up and reduced the cost of emission checks initially. Another example is that of the Delhi government's efforts to decongest residential areas by removing shops located therein have met with a great deal of opposition despite Supreme Court's approval. The scheme had to be modified to mollify the public as well as the affected shopkeepers who did not see much merit in such a drive. Thus 'sealing' of shops had to be either withdrawn or modified to appease the affected people.

Bank customers were earlier happier to see their account details in black and white in a paper passbook. It took a while and some persuasion to overcome the apprehensions of bank customers before changing over to the paperless E-format that could be accessed by the account holder from the safety of his home computer/Internet with a secure user name and password which could be changed as many times as needed by the account holder for the sake of security. Instead of getting the passbook updated every month by an account holder, the one who has opted for paperless transactions via the Internet could access his/her account details any time 24 hours a day any number of times. Such is the convenience that more and more persons, even the skeptics and old timers, are joining the e-bandwagon joyfully as they have realized it's a good idea.

> Those who wish to usher in a change have to do plenty of homework.

The most important point to note is the need to take people into confidence, the earlier the better. Communication should be two-way so that the people have a platform to air their views and see what the reaction is from those who wish to bring a change. Even a simple matter, say, introduction of a one-way street needs involvement of those who are likely to be affected. *One should consider the pros and cons of any change dispassionately*. On the other hand, those who wish to bring in a change in an organization think, "Why should I discuss the proposed change with my people? After all they are being paid for whatever they are supposed to do." Such managers would simply put up a notice board announcing a change. "From next week, we would have one man who would look after two machines instead of one." That would certainly cause resentment from the affected employees. It's likely the labour/employees' union(s), if it exists, would take up cudgels on behalf of the aggrieved employees. They would take up the issue with the management. "If you don't withdraw the order, then you will have to face dire consequences," could be the warning from the union, which wants to fight the order tooth and nail. That could result in go-slow, non-cooperation and even strike to make the management see reason. On its part, the management could take disciplinary actions against agitating employees selectively to 'teach them a lesson' and as a final resort declare a lockout. It is also possible the management sees reason and invites the unions for discussions while putting the proposed order in suspense pending a final outcome.

Let us examine how an understanding manager would have introduced the same change as in the above example. First of all, he would have called a meeting of the employees in his department. He would also invite the shop (union) representative for a frank discussion about the proposed change in the operation system of the machines in order to increase productivity with the principle of 'multi-machine' working for one operator. However, in some units such a discussion would form the agenda in a meeting between the management and the union. Assuming the manager is empowered to take decisions on the introduction of the multi-machine working for operators, the discussion would be confined to the department itself.

Obviously, the employees would raise the question whether some of them would be declared surplus and would be asked to quit or seek voluntary separation. The manager would assure the employees that the management won't retrench anyone but the surplus staff would be relocated without any change in their salaries/wages/perks/benefits. Such an assurance would go a long way in allaying the fears that the management is exploiting them. Moreover, he would offer incentives for the employees who would be working on more than one machine at a time. In such a case, most of the employees would accept the change willingly though some would be unhappy with the relocation of their work elsewhere.

However, if the employees are convinced that the change is good for them as well as the business unit, then the change could be introduced smoothly.

The union too would fall in line when they are convinced that without such a change productivity cannot be improved. If the *status quo* continued, it might result in losses and ultimately closure of the company due to competition. Moreover, the manager would assure the workers, who are called upon to operate more than one machine at a time, that they would be given adequate training, provided proper tools and enhance their existing skills. There would be no penalty for low production during the training period. Such a well thought out plan of introducing a change, with the active participation of the concerned persons, could reduce pangs of change and help in ushering in the change smoothly.

Here are a few tips, see Table below, that could smoothen introduction of change in any milieu:

TABLE

Tips

- Involve the likely affected employees at the earliest stage of planning
- Have frank and open discussion
- Take practical suggestions from the participants
- Have training sessions and remove apprehensions
- Have a trial period
- Remove bugs discovered
- Be a friend and guide to help out those who have problems of adjustment to the change
- There could be initial reluctance/inertia for change. Try to accommodate those who are slow/reluctant change accepters
- Make improvements in the system by taking suggestions from those affected by the change
- Try to unlearn old ideas and practices and think afresh to absorb new ideas and technology

Case Study

A well-known two-wheeler manufacturer in Pune, TRIPLE, manufactured parts for assembly besides buying from reputed vendors. The machine shop produced the parts, which were to be used by the assembly plant. These parts were 100 per cent inspected by the independent inspection department, segregating good and defective parts. Only good parts were sent to the assembly while the defective parts were either reworked or junked. That practice was going on for years. A quality conference was organized for quality control professionals with a visit to the plant. One of the quality professionals from outside asked the managing director who was present at the time of meeting followed by open discussions, "Sir, I notice that the manufacture of parts and inspection of parts are independent of each other. It appears that the responsibility of manufacturing department is to produce parts while another department unconnected with the production is doing sorting. Don't you think that is not the right practice? It's better the sorting would be done by the manufacturing department itself to start with and sorting should be stopped after some time by improving the manufacturing process."

There was stunned silence all around. The quality manager got up and explained that there was nothing wrong in what was happening and the final quality of the two-wheelers was good. "We have been following such a practice for years and we do not see any reason to change the system," averred the quality manager. The managing director was the next to speak. "First of all let me thank the gentleman who gave the suggestion for integrating manufacturing and inspection functions. The suggestion appears sound. In fact, that's the trend all over the advanced world. We shall certainly look into the good idea."

It took a year for the TRIPLE to integrate the manufacturing/inspection functions fully and establish accountability. "Quality first" was the catchy slogan, which was to emphasize that the manufacturing is responsible for what they produce. Moreover, inspection cannot 'build' quality. That was the message that was loud and clear to one and all. The leaders of the labour union too were included in the induction programme to build the kind of environment needed for change, which was seen to be beneficial in the end. The focus shifted to improvement of production process by management actions. In due course of time, with better machines, process and technology, sorting was no longer needed as the parts produced were of acceptable quality. Operators were encouraged to check the parts themselves at random to ensure the quality of parts produced.

> Change should come from the top and should be convincing enough.

No Change—No Progress

The German automaker BMW was producing the *"Beetle"* small car successfully for years and was the favourite of one and all. No one thought beyond a Beetle as it had all the features a driver needed. Then the Japanese came out with innovative models, which were easy on petrol, safer, reliable and priced competitively. The loyal Beetle owners were encouraged by the competitor to try out these Japanese cars. It was a matter of time that the consumers found the Japanese cars more fuel efficient, reliable, with less maintenance and had more features. That was incentive enough for more customers to switch to the Japanese cars. BMW Company watched the situation with dismay and helplessness. What they though "old is gold" proved to be wrong and customers abandoned the much loved, but now discredited, Beetle in favour of shiny Japanese cars. That shows that timely changes are needed to anticipate and face the challenge of competition where everyone wants a share of the pie. *A mere status quo is not good enough in the marketplace.*

The industrial revolution in England and Europe during the mid-1700's spelt the death of cottage industries in India. Machines could produce, what were once painstakingly crafted pieces, many times over much faster and cheaper. Technology improved production process and those who had an edge over it prospered while those still using age-old methods were dumped. They soon lost their market and had to import goods, which they were earlier self-sufficient.

> A study of civilizations reveals a startling similarity. Those who couldn't anticipate and adjust to changes were doomed to decay and destruction.

The invention of gunpowder and automatic weapons spelt the destruction of ancient civilizations in Mexico and South America where once these ancients had made remarkable progress in several fields. But with the advent of the guns, bows and arrows were no match for the destructive power of automatic weapons and that signalled the end of some of the ancient civilizations. Wars are now being waged more and more using the latest technology. For instance ships stationed thousands of miles away from land could launch cruise missiles on enemy territory bang on target with pinpoint accuracy. Cluster bombs and 'monster' bombs deliver deadly ammunition with higher destructive power than earlier. That's why nations in order to defend themselves have no option but to go in for sophisticated weapons that cost much money. Whether a nation should spend so much money on acquiring weapons at the cost of development is a moot time and there is no easy answer.

Case Study

An educational institution already running primary and high schools wanted to start a nursery/pre-school. There was good response, as the building that was built exclusively for the pre-school activity was highly appreciated by the parents. The class-rooms were airy, modern and with all facilities like audio-visual presentation room, library, swimming pool, open spaces for the children to play, clean toilets, attendants to take care of the tiny tots and so on.

The pre-school had trained teachers who took loving care of the children. The modern method was to allow the children to play, sing, draw whatever they liked, but without a formal curriculum. There was no homework to be done back home. Obviously, the children enjoyed their school but the parents were not. They began to complain to the management, "See, madam, my neighbour's child already knows how to write alphabets and recite numericals. How come you are not teaching these simple things to the children in your school?" It took a while for the management to convince the parents that the modern method is not to burden the children with any formal learning but allow them freedom to play and do whatever they wanted. The management assured the parents that the children would certainly be made to learn alphabets, numbers and others in the course of the year but using a different technique that caught the imagination of the kids. "We want children to enjoy learning," clinched the matter. The parents accepted the concept that pre-schooling was a time for the kids to interact with the other children, enjoy playing together, and learn nursery rhymes, identify colours, shapes and so on.

> There is inertia in every human being, whether one likes it or accepts it or not. There is fear of the unknown, which makes matters tougher to accept any change, however laudable it might be intended.

We are comfortable with matters that are known to be steady and reliable. If a change is made that is supposed to improve matters the first question that arises in the minds of the affected is, "Why change for the sake of change? What's wrong with the present status and what's so good with the new fangled change which is supposed to be to our benefit?" Thus there are skeptics who refuse to accept any change that is thrust upon them. The strategy is convincing the people that the change is good and beneficial to them. Thus we have to do a good job of 'selling' an idea before the surprise package is thrust upon the consumers.

Case Study

In a few City Corporations in our country, the Self-Assessment Scheme (SAS) for determining the property tax to be paid every year to the Corporation by property owners was introduced after much homework. Seminars were held, booklets were handed out, examples were shown how to fill up the new form, doubts were cleared, and a trial period of one year was given as grace period. The property owners accepted such planned and transparent introduction of the new scheme, compared to the previous arbitrary corruption-ridden regime of tax inspectors, enthusiastically as it benefitted them. The scheme was hassle-free, open and honest. However, anyone who 'cheated' the system could land himself into trouble as the tax-audit personnel had the right to conduct checks to verify the authenticity of the SAS filed by a householder. Not only that person had to pay a hefty fine but could be penalized too for wrong or wilful incorrect tax returns.

> It's the fear of a change, rather than the change itself that is the root cause of uneasiness.

Sometime people do not think rationally. They fear there could be some ulterior motive where there is none. They need persuasion that the change is for their good, with examples. For instance, if some bank customer is still not keen to get a ATM card, he/she needs to be convinced about the advantages—24-hour banking, no hassles, no waiting, draw money at your convenience, pay by using ATM card after taking proper precaution regarding fraud and so on. Once the customer is convinced, that there are very few risks but many advantages, that person would cautiously start using the ATM card to begin with until he/she is fully convinced that the fear lurking in the mind was mostly imaginary. Some banks have held out a stick—if you do not use the ATM card for drawing cash, you would have to pay a little more money to draw cash through the teller system.

Inertia to Change

Of late banks in the public sector are in the news for the wrong reasons. Instigated by the Labour/Employee Unions, thousands of bank employees, including officers have gone on a strike. The reason is the reluctance on the part of the bank managements to stop a few major changes, which they think would reduce costs, improve efficiency and give better service to the customers. This included merger of some smaller units into bigger banks, off-loading jobs to reduce costs, stop recruitment of staff unless needed and so on. Already, some of the PSU banks have reduced staff through VRS and other incentives. That had become necessary in view of some of the banks in the private sector, including foreign banks, which have pursued clients vigorously and a few of the existing public sector banks customers are slowly, but surely, shifting to the perceived efficient private/foreign banks where they are expected to get International quality service, with more added-value services.

The Labour Unions fear that such major changes are not in the interests of the employees, though they tend to forget the interests of customers without whom the banks do not have a *locus standi*. The unions have spearheaded agitations trying to force the managements give up their plans to restructure and usher in some changes to improve efficiency. It is now a test of will power whether the government would cave in due to agitational tactics of the employees or would continue to pursue the needed changes to bring in modernization and efficiency into the PSU sector banks.

How should two opposing views agree on implementing changes, which improve efficiency and offer better customer satisfaction to the PSU banks customers? That is not easy if both sides stick to their stand come what may. The bank management has the onerous responsibility of convincing the employees and their unions that the changes would not only benefit the customers, strengthen the position of the banks *vis-a-vis* competitors but would benefit the bank employees themselves. That could be 'packaged' in such a manner that the employees/unions would see the brighter side of the proposed changes. For instance, if the retrenchment becomes unavoidable, in order to make the organizations 'lean and mean' then the concerned employees should get a handsome 'golden handshake', which would be attractive enough. Also, the banks should be able to utilize the services of such employees in a suitable manner so that ex-employees could handle the off-loading of certain operations. That would be a 'win-win' situation for both the parties concerned.

Needless Changes

A change introduced to improve quality of life might not be so useful after all. Some skeptics do not endorse a few changes introduced, which are supposed to improve quality of life. Take for example a product like an electric toothbrush. One wonders whether such an 'invention' is really needed wasting so much resource in a gadget that is supposed to replace a simple hand operated toothbrush that has withstood the test of time for centuries. "How does an electric toothbrush improve the quality of life?" the skeptics ask. The moral and ethical question is: "Do we need such changes, which are waste of resources without adding to the quality of life?" It's up to the people to accept a change or not but environmentally conscious persons perhaps would have nothing to do with gadgets which are simply plundering our scarce natural resources. Another example, some might not agree, is the provision of powered-windows, which close or roll down car windows by the touch of a button. Some might explain proudly that it is a wonderful invention, which saves efforts. But others, less enamoured by such inventions, might say, "What's the big deal? Is it such an effort to roll up or down a window by hand?" Moreover, they wonder what would happen if there is a malfunction of the switch or the roll-up/down mechanism or when the battery is low. One has to pay a price for any new gadget but the question is whether such gadgets are really needed or not. Another consideration is whether such (mis) use of resources serves the interest of our environment.

> However, a few changes to reduce pollution, conserve energy and improve efficiency should be welcomed.

For instance, electric cars have a great future if the cost of such vehicles could be brought down and the life of battery could be enhanced to avoid frequent recharging. That is true of hybrid vehicles, which work partly on batteries and fuel. There is a trend towards use of gasohol and ethanol to save petrol and reduce emission of harmful exhaust gases. Similarly, use of 'plastic money' instead of paper money should be adopted sooner or later. Using coins instead of paper currency, for small denominations at least could enhance life of currency.

Those who are keen to change anything that is presently considered usual, routine and time-tested have a job on their hands. First of all, they have a formidable task of changing the mindset of people who are comfortable with the existing system, however inferior it could be. "How do I convince the skeptics?" should be the first question for the change-initiator.

If that person studies the situation carefully, he/she would see a window of opportunity to convince those who are opposed to a change. There is no one solution to a smooth introduction of a change. It has to be tailor-made for each unique situation. In some societies/communities/organizations, there are a few influential leaders who could in turn influence the people under their control. Thus the work of the change-maker becomes easier if he/she could convince these powerful leaders who hold sway over others. In general, there are a few leaders but any followers. So targeting the few leaders could pay off while initiating a change. For instance, if the village panchayat leaders in a village could be convinced on the need to send all the boys and girls of the village to school, then half the battle is won. However, that would mean the local leaders are the first link in the change process.

The need to initiate a change process applies to an organization too where there are leaders, be it union leaders or departmental heads or other powerful individuals with a sizeable following. *The task is to make these persons part of the change initiation process right from the planning to the execution stage.* Such leaders feel honoured, their egos are nursed and they see no threat to their importance in the society/community/organization. In fact they might take the credit for the change themselves, if it proves to be a success. On the other hand, if it is a failure, they could always point a finger elsewhere. *It should be clear that an organization has to reinvent itself to meet challenge of the marketplace otherwise it is doomed to fail miserably.* Any change that is introduced should be for the improvement in the working of the organization and to satisfy its customers with cheaper and better quality products and services.

> Changes, be it in the organization, machines, equipments, technology or process, should be planned in advance as it is better to do so when time is on one's side rather than try to catch up with the competition in a crisis.

Case Study

A few States have introduced compulsory wearing of helmets for two-wheeler riders and pinion riders. The success of such a move is mixed, with some States enforcing the rule strictly while others are not too keen to enforce with the fear that it would alienate a sizeable section of the population. A law that is supposed to protect the head of riders in case of an accident is meeting resistance. "We are not used to a helmet", "It makes us feel very hot", "My hair gets spoiled", "A helmet is too heavy and impairs my vision", "A helmet is expensive", "I can protect my head. It's up to me", and so on are the litany of complaints when authorities force the riders to wear the helmet while riding. Those who want to fool the policemen wear the helmet but do not buckle it, which voids the benefit of wearing a helmet for protection. Others keep the helmet on the vehicle or give it to the pillion rider to wear it or keep it in case a policeman suddenly appears on the scene demanding why the rider is not wearing the helmet.

There are so many ingenious ways of fooling the system when riders are not convinced that the change is for their own good and not to please anyone.

Confronted with a stiff opposition to the helmet rule, the authorities are in a fix. "See, by wearing a helmet the accidental death rate has reduced by more than half. So please start wearing helmets for your own sake," appeal is not cutting much ice with the riders who think their head is safe. Doctors too vouch for the fact that helmet is a protection that saves lives. In sharp contrast is the situation in advanced countries where even a child riding bicycle wears a helmet for protection without anyone telling him/her to wear it. The reason is the high level of awareness regarding safety, which we lack in our country.

How does anyone bring in the change so that riders voluntarily wear helmets? That is not easy, as the inertia and mindset have to change over a period of time. By making the wearing of helmet 'optional' is not going to help much as riders are still not convinced about the usefulness of the helmet and tout all sorts of excuses for not wearing one.

> For ushering in the change, a mass awareness campaign blitz needs to be launched throughout the state.

Every leader, from every field of activity, including celebrities, should be roped in to spread the message that a helmet saves life. In the beginning no penalty should be levied on those who do not wear a helmet. *People need time to adjust to the new change over a period*. However, the campaign for use of a helmet has to be innovative, sustained and involve the people. They need to be convinced that a helmet is for their benefit and not of anyone else. Statistics should be displayed prominently how many people died or seriously injured over a period of time when they were not wearing a helmet.

If the authorities, not swayed by political/popular pressure stand firm, a change such as the above that is in the larger interest of the public could be implemented over a time, with minor adjustments, if necessary. The problem arises when a change is introduced with a feeling it is going to be unpopular and such a rule might lose votes for the party in power. Such narrow considerations are not in the interest of the public who should be guided properly. The onus is on the government to make the change as painless and hassle free as possible by doing a thorough home work and anticipate all the problems that might arise during the implementation of the intended change. For instance, good quality helmets priced reasonably should be available at various outlets so that people could buy these. It is recommended that people are involved as early as possible in the proposed change that should be shown as beneficial to the public at large and there is no hidden agenda either. People take time to absorb a change but once they are convinced they would like to have similar changes that benefits them directly or indirectly.

Change management, be it in ordinary life or in an organization should be thought about carefully and should be well planned for a smooth implementation. The more detailed the pre-planning is done the better for a smoother introduction of the change, without tears.

Change, however well intentioned, is likely to be resisted, sometimes just for the sake of opposing. A change has to have some meaning to those who are asked to fall in line with the change. The "What's In It For Me" (WIIFM) factor is obviously strong. An individual should see something good coming out by adopting/adapting to the change quickly and willingly. For instance, that a voter should have an ID for voting is a sound idea and that is being introduced to prevent bogus votes being cast. An individual would be convinced that no one could vote in his/her name if the electoral official demands a photo ID card that gives details of the voter as also his/her picture.

> There should be less coercion and more persuasion while introducing a change.

That is because any change that is forced down the throat of a person will be resisted and accepted half-heartedly. On the other hand, if the change were packaged well and attractively, then more people who are likely to be affected by the proposed change would accept such a change enthusiastically. That is the secret recipe for change management that should be learnt by everyone, including managers. Moreover, give the people time to settle down to the newly introduced change and penalty should be avoided, as it would leave a bitter taste in the affected persons that the management is in a hurry and is not human at all. Changing people's perception and mindset are the most important aspects to be considered for any one desiring to introduce a change.

> Change is inevitable, be it at the workplace or in society.

That could be due to a natural process or in response to a challenge. Inertia is a powerful force that thwarts attempts to change. The fact is people are comfortable with old well tried and simple methods and resent it if something sophisticated and complicated method, procedure, rule or law is thrust upon them suddenly even without consulting them. They are hesitant to accept anything that is new or novel because of some irrational fear. Hence the change seekers should make matters simpler and as painless as possible for the people to accept a change voluntarily. Once people accept the change and get used to it slowly, it is matter of time they are comfortable with working with the changed scenario. In fact, they could be on the look for changes, once they are confident of successfully adapting to a change that improves their quality of life.

A change that is seen as beneficial and good by the change-seeker should also be seen so by the people who are asked to accept the change. What is important is that a change-seeker should not be in a hurry to introduce a change but should consider all the problems and difficulties likely to be faced by the affected. Suppose, the government decides to stop printing of short denominations notes like Rupees one, two and five, the logic of coins as replacement should be explained to the consumers at large that it would be cheaper for everyone in the long-run as compared to paper currency. The government should have already arranged for adequate supply of coins even before the change from paper to coins is introduced. It is the ability of the change-seeker to make people, likely to be affected by the change, comfortable that is the hallmark of a good change, be it in an organization or society. *People should not be hassled into a change just because the leaders want to take credit for ushering in the change.* Moreover, it is easier to focus on tangible things rather than any abstract matter that is hard to comprehend by the people in general.

> We are in a dynamic world, which is ever changing. Managing change is a challenge and an opportunity that could benefit the people. That is the only way of taking people along on the path of progress by making them part of the change process.

8

Organization

—For orderly conduct of business

Whether a nation or a business is concerned, a structured organization is *sine qua non* for orderly conduct and to ensure success. In the ancient Greek nation, each city-state was independent and democratic way of life was enshrined with the active and wholehearted cooperation of the citizens. Even in a free and democratic nation a number of laws and rules are needed for orderly conduct of its citizens. Such an effort can be seen in the structure of an organization too. Every organization worth its name has a CEO, Chief Executive Officer, who can go under various names—chairman, president, and so on. It is up to the CEO to have his/her own organization that suits the need of business. Large Corporations are in place, be it MNCs (Multi-National Companies) are domestic giants with a large number of employees under their control. There is no unique organization structure that suits every business. An organization that is not well defined is in trouble one way or the other as it gives loopholes for people to manipulate such an organization.

However, smaller business units reporting to a centralized office has become the norm due to their flexibility and at the same time with support from a corporate office for major decisions like budget, investment, merger, take-over and long-term planning.

> The trend is to have lesser number of layers of control compared to a rigid hierarchical structure. Such an organization is known as a "Horizontal Organization" compared to a traditional one with rigid top-down control.

HORIZONTAL ORGANIZATION

In these days of liberalization and globalization, the trend is to have leaner horizontal organizations with fewer chains of command. The category of 'supervisor' is fast becoming an endangered species. People like to be supervised less. They want responsibility and willing to take it, if only a management trusts its people. In fact, some employees might even ask for it. In such organizations, the very concept of a 'boss' is getting outdated. It's the team that delivers not any individual, at least that's the theory. However, reality is different. People work for the team (the organization) and at the same time they work for themselves too. There is nothing wrong in such an attitude provided there are lesser conflicts of interests between the self and the organization. It's the overarchical ambition of a few individuals, which causes problems to an organization.

Under the regime of a less top-heavy set-up, to expect a member of a team to get promoted regularly would be difficult. However, there is a way out. Those who deserve to be recognized might end up with cash and other incentives. That is not much of a consolation for those who want to climb the hierarchical ladder. Some organizations re-designate those who are promoted using labels such as 'systems analyst', 'group leader', 'group-manager', 'project-manager', 'deputy manager', and 'director'. In such promotions, the team structure and chain of command remain more or less the same to avoid heart burning in those who have been overlooked for promotion or recognition. That is better than humiliating people by putting one person, a colleague at that, as the boss to whom every team member reports. Nevertheless, there would be unhappiness still all around with such designations, though under-current and subtle, but people are likely to recognize that the management has done a deft balancing act in lieu of many conflicting factors.

An organization, mostly in the software IT business has fewer layers of command and less number of designations. The under mentioned organizational structure shows one possible structure, though details could vary depending upon the size/complexity of business.

Organizational Structure

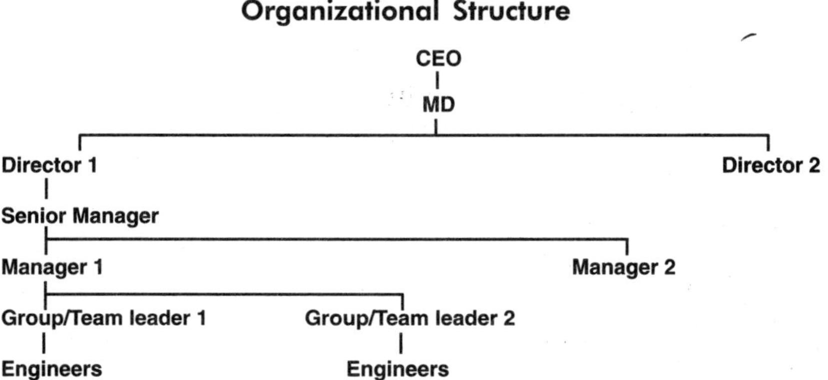

Job Designations

An organization has many jobs to be performed by people, though often a senior manager holds more than one function to coordinate and to lead. The job descriptions are not standardized though some commonality could be found when scanning through various organizations, which have carried on successful business for decades. Some of the job descriptions that organizations use to designate their managers/supervisors/employees could be seen from the list given below though by no means complete and exhaustive:

CEO
MD
GM, Chief GM, deputy GM, senior GM
Director
Project Manager
Departmental Head
Development Manager/Analyst
Development Executive
Administrator
Business Development Executives
Programme Executive/Analyst
Senior Technical Architect
Web designer
Junior Programmer
Accounts Manager/administrative manager/accounts assistants
Stores manager
Fashion designer
Senior Quality Controller
Regional Manager/senior manager/manager/plant manager
Sales engineer/manager/personnel manager
Law officers
Professor/Assistant professors/lecturers
Principal/Reader
Investment consultants
Chief Manager (Marketing)
Management Trainee
Chartered accountant/chief accountant
Engineer/manufacturing engineer/structural engineer/quality engineer/engineer project management
Inspectors
Branch managers/divisional manager
Field officer
System programmer
Supervisors

Customer relation manager
Chief project manager
Secretary
HR coordinator
Senior Analyst
Manager-Business Development
Senior Developer
Team Leader
Solution Architect
Assistant Manager/Manager Recruitment
Technical Sales Specialist

Traditional Organization

Certain organizations, even now, are top-heavy with a clear indication of who reports to whom. No doubt that is a traditional hierarchical organization where it is the "top-down" approach to managing an organization. The power centers are clearly defined with one person reporting to another and so on. The belief in such an organization is that with the clarity in the chain of command, as could be seen in the army, church and other such organizations, work becomes easier and any problem could be resolved by timely intervention of the person higher up the ladder. That is more so in a family run business where 'outsiders', even now, are looked upon with suspicion, unless the CEO is broad-minded enough to take such 'outsiders' into confidence in managing the family-run business. That is where professionalism in family-run business could prove advantageous with infusion of outside talent.

> There is a certain degree of evolution of an organization as it grows or shrinks.

Often, a few functions are combined for better coordination but at other times it would be in the interest of the organization that a certain function is independent of a particular department. For instance, Quality Control/Assurance/Audit are important functions and should be as independent as possible so that the management gets an unbiased view of the important function of quality that directly affects customer satisfaction. However, process quality control which used to be part of a quality control set-up is now generally attached to the manager in charge of production so that he/she could get feedback on quality during process. In fact, such an arrangement would put the onus of quality on the production/ manufacturing department since it has access to information on quality of product/process during manufacture itself.

A typical traditional organization could be as shown in the next page. Designations/number of positions vary depending upon the nature of business as well complexity.

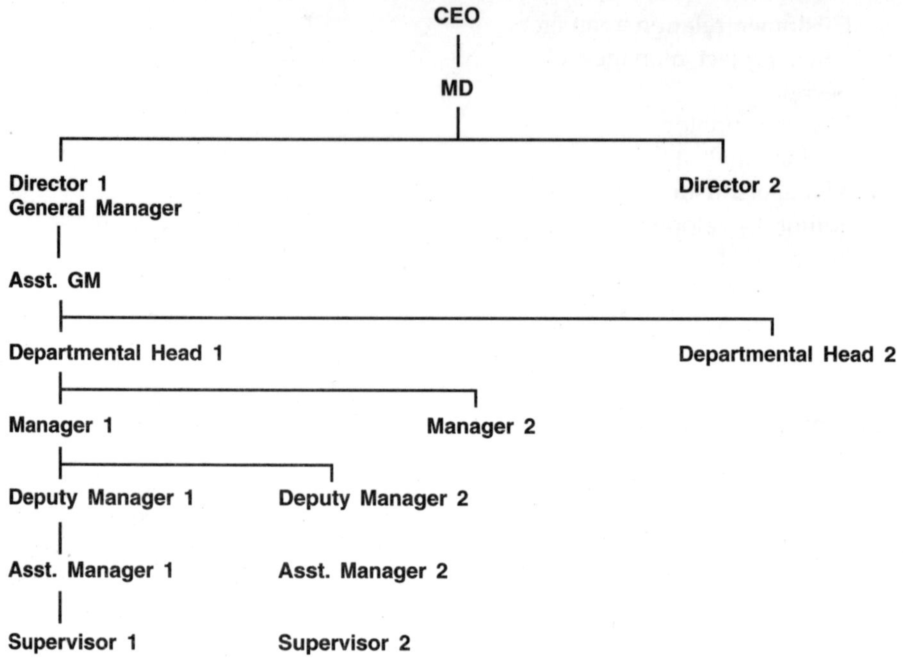

A point that needs to be noted in the above organizational structures is there are certain functions, which have to be there for the success of the business. These are: Accounts, Administration, Human Resources Department (HRD), Materials Management (Purchase and vendor assistance), Quality Audit/Certification, Quality Control/Assurance, Security, Training, Transport and so on. Some of these functions could under one director/general manager depending on the organization.

Our Public Sector Units (PSUs) are top heavy.

There are too many layers in PSU management. So an average employee does not even know to whom he/she is working. That is the problem with huge organizations. Some of these posts were created for specific persons and these remain still open though some of them have ceased to have any meaning. For instance, Class IV employees, who do all sorts of lowly jobs and are poorly paid, are not needed if only the employees do their own work—dusting, getting files, dispatching, catering to the food/drinks of employees, running errands and so on. Thus the PSUs, and some private sector companies, have created organizations, which are inefficient. However, any attempt to restructure the organizations meet with stiff resistance as the employees/labour/employee union(s) resist such attempts. *They are more concerned with job security and employment potential than improving efficiency of the organization*. A similar fate awaits time and motion study reports that would tell the management certain jobs could be done differently or even drastically curtailed to improve overall efficiency. Wastage of resource(s), including human asset, has to receive better attention if the efficiency of the organization has to show improvement.

Business Units for Better Management

Often when a company/organization grows rapidly, a stage is reached when it becomes unwieldy for easy control as well as to coordinate the activities of so many departments/disciplines/functions. "Let us have a maximum of 1000 employees in our unit," specifies a CEO which would mean such a small unit is viable though certain common functions like administration, canteen, HRD, purchase, transport and so on might have to be duplicated when the big unit splits into smaller business units. However, experts opine that is a small price to pay for a small robust efficient unit that could stand on its own and fight competition better. It would focus on its business objective better than a big unit, which has diversified into several products/business as it expanded without much thought to control, cost, efficiency or flexibility.

The advantage of a small business unit is that it is easily manageable. Each department is small and the manager of each department could vibe with his/her team members better. The boss could have a first name relation with the staff members in the department, which helps building bridges of understanding and cooperation. Each member of the team knows to whom he/she is working compared to a large department which is so unwieldy that people lose their individuality and become a mere cog in the process of business/process/production. It is also possible that each employee could be trained for a multitude of functions to improve flexibility when the need arises. There is a personal touch in the small units that helps bonding with each other in the larger interests of the business unit.

Case Study

One of the multi-national companies in Pune went in for expansion of its Pune plant. What was once only a few hundred employees became a big unit with several product-wise manufacturing units working almost independently. When the unit strength became 3000 employees, there were discussions whether the unit should expand even further. Those who felt the unit was viable won the day. The argument was that certain functions like administration, finance, transport, and personnel departments housed under one roof saved costs. The convincing argument was the unit was still manageable. Another powerful argument was the radio assembly and the electronic measuring equipments assembly which got parts from their own captive production unit located within the factory was able to perform well with little delays, greater flexibility and very little transportation costs.

When the director of the MNC in-charge of South-East Asia came, arguments were put forth for maintaining the *status quo,* and in fact even a proposal for further expansion of the same plant, as space was no problem, a point forcefully put forth by the plant in-charge. However, the director, an experienced person with a wide knowledge of organization structures around the globe explained the rationale of having smaller viable Business Units (BUs), a trend all over the world. The explanation was simple: "Small is beautiful". Though initially more investment was needed by way of building infrastructure, the effort, he explained, was worth the extra expenditure in the long-run. He wanted these units to grow to a reasonable size, say, a maximum of 1000 employees, and if it became bigger, again split into a smaller units in the larger interest of making the BU not only profitable but an accountable one too. It was explained further that it would be easier to manage the workforce as well as production and logistical issues better than a mega-unit.

That was also the (part) logic when the unit of Indian Telephone Industries Ltd., a pioneer in Telecommunication in the earlier years located in Bangalore, had grown bigger and had to be split into smaller units when at its peak the staff strength was 30,000, with a township for the people coming in as a bonus. However, when further expansion was required, there was a clamour for setting up telecommunication units in other parts of the country like Kerala and Uttar Pradesh. That was part political too as the concerned States wanted industrialization to take place within their boundaries. So Public Sector Units were set-up in other parts of the country, which was a good thing from the point of view of establishing smaller viable units and also as a means of improving the employment potential of various states. However, the main unit at Bangalore diversified but found competition too tough to handle and had to be downsized over the years to a shadow to what it was in those halcyon years.

How to usher in a change is a matter of deep concern discussed in a separate chapter. We have to overcome the mindset of not only the management staff but that of the employees too. The managers feel that by restructuring they are losing their importance and feel more comfortable with the *status quo*. However, if the change could be shown that benefits them, then more people would be amenable for the proposed change. The WIIFM (What's In It For Me) factor is important and has to be built into any scheme that proposes to improve overall efficiency of the set-up.

Cross-functional Teams

Much has been debated about compartmentalizing departments that help a unit to work better since they are sharply focused on their target. There is often a rigid boundary separating one department from the other. *That was the tradition of older units, though such units exist even now, a relic of the Taylor principle of dividing work among various departments to maximize work output and boost efficiency*. However, that type of dividing work among departments, created barriers for better inter-departmental relationships. "It's not our work. That belongs to another department," was the common refrain when a problem arose between departments. Unfortunately, one faces a similar situation in certain governmental and semi-governmental organizations even now where employees work to a set of rigid rules. It appears that the departments work for themselves rather than for the good of the total organization for which the various departments are part and parcel. Thus, inter-departmental coordination became the bottleneck for better coordination and successful work culture, with customer focus. It is a tough task to break such work habits and make the department see the larger picture. That was not easy given the fact that the departments were given a target and each one of them was keen to complete it ahead of others to prove how efficient they were.

While breaking down a unit into various manageable departments/ sub-units that facilitate work, a fair degree of inter-departmental cooperation/coordination is a must to resolve mutual problems quickly and efficiently. "Cross-functional teams" are the answer for resolving inter-departmental problems.

In such a team every one is equal, though there could be one person designated for keeping record and for better coordination within and outside the departments concerned. Each concerned department, however remotely connected with a problem, nominates one person, fairly senior and well trained in problem-solving techniques for the team which has a specific mandate-tackle only one problem given to it at a time.

Normally, once the team completes the project successfully and its report accepted, the team is 'dissolved'. *Such teams have the advantage that personalities are out and the problem is focused by all the team members.* Some bias cannot be helped especially by those who are directly affected by the problem. There could be an attempt to shield the department, as the concerned departmental people do not want to be seen in a poor light. However, the senior managers should assure the team that resolving the inter-departmental problem is more important than assigning blame to any one. Such assurance could put the team members at easy and give out their best to find a quick acceptable solution in the larger interests of the organization. *The idea should be to find out not who is wrong but what's wrong.* A case study of how an inter-departmental problem was handled and solved successfully by a cross-functional team is detailed elsewhere in another chapter.

The onus is on the CEO and the senior managers to emphasize the fact that the organization is bigger than any one department. Though employees belong to one or another department in an organization, each and every employee should feel that the overall goals of the organization has to be given prominence rather than attaining any one department's set goals. For example, if a customer has genuine complaint about a product/service, the person to whom the customer complains should have the responsibility of conveying the message to the right person himself rather than pass the buck to some other department/person. He/she might be working within rules but the customer gets a poor opinion about such an organization which is seen as not so customer-friendly. That is true of any matter of interest affecting the public/government/environment where each and every employee has to shoulder some responsibility and see that the problem is solved amicably and quickly.

Management without Controls

It would be ideal if all the employees, at all levels, understand and carry out their allocated work efficiently with no supervision. Everyone would be then be a person who handles responsibility without anyone telling him/her or supervising that person's work. However, such a Utopian environment is hard to find in medium/big enterprises but for the smallest one where there are fewer staff members to carry on the various aspects of a business. However, empowerment of employees is going on briskly. The idea is to encourage employees to learn multi-tasking and be able to fill the gap when some one is absent. No longer employees dare to state, "But that's not my work." In this fast changing world the employees are required to accept responsibility willingly for not only the good of the company but for themselves too. In fact, there is a selfish reason too—the employee is eying greener pastures elsewhere all the time. So the better he/she is adaptable to a work situation the better for 'marketing' him/her self, when the need arose.

Delegation is one way of making a junior person handle a future responsibility with confidence. The boss tries to groom up that person with the expectation he/she would rise to the occasion and then he/she would become 'surplus.' *Bringing up subordinates is one way an organization grows when the baton is handed over to someone who is younger*. Some large companies decide that the CEO after he/she reaches the age, say 65 or 70 years, would retire and then the suitable successor is chosen who is next in line. That CEO who is about to retire is offered a place as 'mentor' if that person so desires otherwise he/she is happy to carry on doing something different during his/her (productive) life after retirement.

> An organization expects its employees to show initiative and come forward voluntarily to accept challenges. That could be in the form of taking up additional responsibilities and or multi-tasking.

Youngsters want a job that is challenging so that they could prove their worth. An organization has to give opportunities to youngsters so that they are not frustrated due to lack of challenges. Often, merely getting more money or taking up higher level in an organization is not motivating enough for some employees. They want challenges and they would, like to prove they could do it with little help from the management. Such is the confidence some youngsters have in themselves.

"Work is worship" is the motto for a few employees who could be labelled as *karmayogis*. They do not expect any rewards for succeeding in their work. Completion of a project successfully is all the reward they expect. However, if the management and the peers appreciate their work, they are more than happy. However, they do not look for applause when they complete their allotted work successfully ahead of time. True, we have very few such *karmayogis* who are selfless and above any reward system. But for the majority of employees, a pat on the back, praising them openly by managers and some sort of recognition/award/reward system is still of interest. *Interestingly, sometimes such an award becomes a non-motivator due to the fact that the majority of employees do not see any merit in such an award.* That is the reason why an award/reward has to be honest and transparent and should be perceived so by the majority of the employees, if such a system has to motivate others to strive for higher levels of performance.

> The culture of an organization plays a big part in the way excellence is recognized and rewarded. That could be one of the biggest motivators for fostering excellence.

On the one hand we have companies that are miserly that rarely appreciate the work of their employees however outstanding it might have been. Their philosophy is simple—'Anyway what's so great about that employee's work? We expect every employee to perform well. After all, we pay them well, you know." That is a cynical way of berating an employee's contribution to the organization. At the other end of the spectrum, we have companies who take every opportunity to praise their employees in a genuine and open manner. All significant contributions by individuals are recognized at various fora. Those with outstanding contributions are honoured with certificate of merit/best employee of the month/cash and other incentives. In such an organization employees really look forward to recognition of their work by the management, as they know the organization is sincere in appreciating their contributions. Often an employee wishes, when he/she had a bad day in the workplace/office that there was no organization and no boss to nitpick. Such an attitude is natural as work is stressful. The boss could make a difference by being understanding and not by merely demanding a task that it should be completed according to a time schedule. What the employee wants that he/she should be taken into confidence before any schedule is decided. Sometimes, a customer wants a product within a fixed time frame. It would be then the duty of everyone to pitch in and see that the work is completed on time and according to the highest quality norms for the product/service. A customer might excuse a slight delay but not a shoddy product that fails to meet stringent standards of quality laid down by the customer as that could prove to be embarrassing. *The more the involvement of the concerned employees in planning and executing a project the better so that people are self-motivated and the need for chasing employees to speed up work becomes redundant.*

Flexible Hours

Organizations are allowing women employees to work from home. That is a trend that is picking up. However, even then the concerned employees are required to put in their presence for a few 'core hours' at the office/workplace so that there could be meaningful interaction between the manager and his/her staff which is partly working from home. That indeed is a novel way of utilizing workforce while giving them freedom to work with flexible hours. With Internet, Video-conferencing and other latest technology, it is possible to keep in touch with the employees though at far away destinations. For instance, a few companies in the USA have set-up overseas sites for better productivity, low cost and spread of operations to cater to area specific clients. The manager-in-charge in the US would then have a bank of computers in his/her office and access the person(s) through telephones for clarifications and updating progress of a project.

Part-time employees are not rigidly bound by organizational constraints of working fixed hours say nine to five. That is a great boon to women employees as well as senior citizens who do not wish to commute long distances day in and day out to attend offices/workplaces right on time while facing family problems, traffic jams, bad weather and the like. Some of these employees, also those working flexible hours, do not mind a smaller take-home pay for the sheer convenience of working when they want and not because they have to work for their living. Organizations that depend upon a pool of part-time/flexible hour employees are a happy lot too. In fact some companies do not mind if some of the senior employees/managers retire voluntarily early. However, those who wish to work from home or join the offices/workplaces after retirement could do so when the peak work demands which could be seasonal. *These organizations are doing a great job of offering employees "work when they want" while retaining their goodwill.*

More such alternate work arrangements could follow when a few employees do not wish to be tied down to work forgetting all their other social and family responsibilities in life. In fact, certain countries offer paternity leave to the husband when the wife is delivering a baby or when the baby is too young. The organization wants the employee to be with the wife and help her out while still on their payroll. Such humane considerations could go a long way in cementing good relations between the employees and the organization, which could be looked upon as a father figure. Some organizations offer an employee a 'sabbatical' leave of absence with full pay, for one to two years when that person has put in a certain number of years of service with the company. Such an employee is free to do whatever he/she wants—study, take up another assignment, offer volunteer service, travel, spend time with the family when the need arises, for example when the spouse or child is seriously sick.

> Organizations will have to innovate to utilize the talent of a large pool of skilled and semi-skilled persons for not only their own benefit but also help the people of the community to generate incomes.

Working from home, using flexible hours to attract women and other employees, farming out jobs/tasks to small self-help groups and using physically challenged persons optimally would be some of the innovative methods that organizations might deploy to tap the talent pool while remaining profitable. A few organizations wishing to be flexible in their work, form smaller groups within an organization who could turn out products profitably without too much overheads and elaborate procedures. For example, if a valuable customer wants a few pieces of a product, say one hundred as a one-off production, a large company might not go out of the way to help that customer as it would be too expensive for not only itself but the consumer too to work on such small quantities at any one time. Under these conditions, organizations could think of setting up smaller captive units that cater to small-scale batch production. The large organization would then concentrate only on large volumes to remain profitable. That could be done under its own umbrella or entrust the work to its own small-scale vendors who would execute such jobs easily at lower cost.

Case Study

In a medium size unit in Pune the company decided to end the provision of transport to its officers by requesting the drivers to accept voluntary separation. The officers had to engage their own driver or drive the vehicle himself, if he wished so. The costs could be reimbursed or included in the pay packet as vehicle allowance. However, the company offered the cars to the drivers at a discount with financial arrangement for those unable to purchase the vehicles. In return, the drivers were bound to report at the gate every morning or be on call when needed, so that their vehicles could be used by the company's officers/employees when needed. If the company did not need their services for that day, the drivers who were then the owners of the vehicles were free to offer their services elsewhere. Such an arrangement was a 'win-win' situation for the company as well as the drivers.

An organization is a means of orderly conduct of a business profitably. It generally evolves over the years keeping its needs in mind. Change is inevitable and an organization, small, medium or big, has to change keeping in mind the market trends. A rigid structure cannot work efficiently as the people give priority to a set of rules rather than keeping the organizational goal in mind—that of *customer satisfaction*. Thus innovation in the structure of an organization to meet the competition and be in tune with the market/global trends is an on-going exercise.

Mergers and Acquisitions

The UK-based "Steel King" Lakshmi Mittal has created history by acquiring many steel plants across the globe. He has bid successfully, some of the units in the red, to build a steel empire that few could challenge. The trend to acquire companies is not new. However, in view of the WTO regime, nations are obliged to allow mergers and acquisitions easier than before. National borders are shrinking which is a boost to world free trade with tariff barriers coming down drastically.

The idea to acquire units under one management is to make products available cost-effectively. That is possible due to the advantages of economy of scale. Distribution of products of high quality is another plus point with one unit controlling manufacture and distribution. Some companies have been following the principle of setting specific units for products to make production costs lower by sheer scale of production. For example, one MNC had set-up a colour TV factory in Singapore, which became a world production centre for TV, though it could franchise the product to other nations to make production/distribution easier.

> Mergers and acquisitions/takeovers are not painless.

Some degree of retrenchment becomes inevitable, as the new management wants to make the company 'lean and mean'. However to allay the fears of employees of a company, which is being bought by another, an assurance is given that there would not be large-scale retrenchment but employees could be relocated if the need arises.

Sometimes a merger means no change in the brand name. For instance, Jet Airlines bought Sahara Airlines but some of the aircraft carry the same logo of the erstwhile Sahara. That applies to Air Deccan, which is now part of the Kingfisher brand. Air Deccan maintains its own brand name as well as its low fares. However, a few functions like aircraft maintenance and some other logistical issues could be handled by one organization that would make the unit more profitable. That is also the idea when there is code sharing by various airlines to offer customers better service across a wider network.

To keep a brand name (say A) visible the company (say B) that takes it over would like to keep it the same (A) to retain brand loyalty. In such an event employees get a better deal when a big company takes over a smaller unit. However, mergers are not generally welcomed by stakeholders/ employees/labour unions as they fear retrenchment and loss of job opportunity as well as loss of brand identity. Again, that company which wants to take over should assuage the feelings of employees as well as stakeholders. The Public Sector Banks are in the process of consolidation which is not welcomed by the employees/unions as they fear loss of jobs and job opportunities. They are resorting to strikes in protest and force the bank managements to abandon plans for mergers or privatization. Such a confrontation perhaps could be avoided if both sides settle contentious issues through dialogue. The case study pertaining to such an issue is detailed in another chapter.

Unorganized Sector

What is not appreciated is the fact that we have millions of workers in the unorganized sector who do not have access to benefits of the organized sector. Most of the small-scale units are a one-man show, which are interested only in making money. Some of them could be categorized as 'fly-by-night' operators who could vanish in a jiffy by swindling the employees/ customers/government. In small-scale units workers are not paid their wages regularly and benefits are minimal. What the actual take home pay of workers could be different from what appears in the book to swindle the workers as well as the government. 'Hire-and-fire' policy is the norm in the unorganized sector where the organization structure is simple—the boss orders and everyone obeys. A loyal senior worker could double up as the next in the pecking order but with little powers of decision-making.

Most of them do not have any professionalism in their management. The infrastructure is poor, with no proper lighting or ventilation. Outdated equipments are still in use. Pollution control is largely forgotten, as they do not wish to invest in costly control equipment. However, whether one likes it or accepts it or not, the unorganized sector provides employment to millions of people, contributes taxes, adds to the GDP and helps the organized sector to benefit from low cost inputs made by that sector. However, there is a crying need to bring professionalism into the management of these small-scale units. The employees, though not organized into unions, deserve better wages and some benefits at least. The government should help the small-scale units to help themselves while taking care to see that their employees are treated fairly and get at least the minimum wages, leave facility, and benefits like PF, gratuity, under the Labour Act.

9

Corporates

—Dreaming big

Corporations, at least some of them, have earned a bad name because they bend the rules and think they could get away with anything with their influence/money power. However, due to public and governmental pressure, matters are slowly, but surely, changing for the better. There is now a greater awareness that corporates have to be ethical, stick to governmental regulations including environmental rules and laws, give a fair deal to the employees, stakeholders and the vendors. Profit is no doubt the motive of any business but that should be ethical and above board. Of late corporations are on a buying, selling, merger, acquisitions, and take-over mode. Some of the largest corporations are trying to pool their resources together for better reach and profitability. For instance, the move by a few airlines like Air France and Swiss Air to take over Alitalia, the ailing Italian carrier, is a case in point. However, the Italian Government has bailed it out temporarily by providing funds for its operating expenses. We in our country too have seen mergers to consolidate companies in the airlines business, for instance, the merger of Airlines Jet and Sahara, Kingfisher and Air Deccan. Tata Motors have purchased two luxury models of Ford Motor Company, Jaguar and Land Rover, by paying US $ 2.3 billion, which has made big news (2008).

Unfortunately, big corporations have run into big problems, some of which are of their own making. Their public relations are poor and secrecy surrounds their activities, some of which are not in the public interest.

> The more transparent and ethical a corporation is the better to infuse confidence in the employees, stakeholders, vendors, NGOs and public at large.

Some charitable foundations started by enlightened corporate giants like Bill Gates are doing yeoman service to the society by investing in activities that would improve the quality of life of the sick and the underprivileged. That matter is assuming greater importance than before, as a corporate is judged not merely by its bottom line but also by its commitment to social/community/environmental causes.

ACHIEVING BIG

"Doing business today takes guts, knowledge, skill, and insight. If you have got the guts, we can help you with the rest. You can become the architect of something big, something bold, and something completely new. There has never been a more exciting time to be in business. Come on let us get started," states an advertisement blurb for the magazine Harvard Business that reflects the business milieu of modern times. Competing across borders requires out-of-the-box strategies as the world is shrinking. With stiff competition, domestic as well as foreign, companies have to shed their old ways of thinking and doing. *They need new tools to leverage value inside a company*. The recent (2007-08) rupee appreciation *vis-a-vis* US dollar has put pressure on the margins and corporates have to think of innovative solutions to keep their bottom line healthy and strong. They have to reduce costs, innovate products and find alternate customers.

The importance of corporations can never be exaggerated given the fact that they contribute to the national economy besides employing lakhs of people. Their contribution towards community development has received better attention than ever before. Thanks to some of the enlightened Corporations, the quality of life of the employees and their families has improved over the years. A few governmental controls are necessary in any free economy but these are aimed at controlling unhealthy and fraudulent practices that harm the economy as well as those who invest in the corporations as stakeholders. Ethical behaviour of corporations is under the scanner and there is public pressure, also through shareholders, that they conduct themselves in a manner that is straightforward without resorting to dubious methods to show a healthy bottom-line or go one-up on another corporation. Every corporation in India wants to make it big to spread its influence around the globe to make 'Brand India' a household name all over the world just like a few International well known brands.

The late Dhirubhai Ambani of Reliance is a shining example how a small time operator could build an industrial empire par excellence. No doubt, he had a slice of luck and utilized the right opportunities at the right time. But that in no way could take away the outstanding leadership quality of a man who had barely an education, with none from a professional college. What he had in abundance was his dream to make it big come what may. He overcame hurdles after hurdles to build an organization where the employees and the stakeholders took pride in belonging to the Reliance Family, a label to be cherished.

His was an inspiration, which propelled the team to greater heights. He wanted his men to make Reliance not only a big organization in India but one of the biggest in the world. That was his vision, which, luckily for him, could happen during his lifetime. Although finance was important, which he could collect through loyal and enthusiastic investors, he treated the people as assets. He had the foresight to scout around and have the best talent he could gather. They were a set of loyal professionals who were constantly reminded about his dream to make Reliance 'big and best'. People too shared his dream. He set higher and higher goals but, importantly, provided them the means to achieve the higher goals, through motivation, training, skill enhancement, and technology up-gradation. We should remember: "Success stories don't just happen. They are made",— Bosch. With the world shrinking the time has to think big with a "Global vision".

Employees need to be trusted fully in whatever they do. They resent a boss who interferes too much with their work—after all, they need space to operate and put in their own thoughts on the job on hand to satisfy their ego needs. *While one is in pursuit of excellence there is no scope for compromise.* "Dream it big," is what a leader has to remind the people around him. However, it cannot happen by mere platitudes. The leader has to support the people fully and create an environment *where excellence is a way of life*. In such a place, shoddy work has no place. Employees themselves would reject any such compromise knowing fully that the customer might not accept even one defect. As a CEO stated: "We have very, very talented people who have to subordinate their ego to become part of a team."—Llloyd Craig Blankfein, Chairman & CEO, Goldman Sachs. We're not relying on the world staying the same and we're not relying on all conditions being good.

> What is generally not appreciated is the fact that people could rise above their own self-imposed limits.

Management should provide the motivation and an environment where success is rewarded, and more importantly, failures are not held over some one as a black mark. Such a person too needs to be given a pat on the back for making sincere and serious efforts to achieve the goal. Otherwise, disenchantment might set in and that person might not have the desire to try harder since he is not sure of the success. If the sailing is smooth then achieving a goal might not be so tough. *What is important is for the team to work purposely towards the goal set under trying and difficult circumstances.* When the chips are down the employees need moral and emotional support from the top managers. Suppose the unit is facing a tough competition in the market that is not the time to throw in the towel and give up. In fact, the employees would have to pull together as never before and face the competition head-on.

> Each employee has a potential waiting to be tapped.

Given the generally adversarial relation between the employee and the boss there is not much of an opportunity for the employee to blossom. That is because a smart employee is seen as a threat to the position of the immediate boss. So he will do his best to put all sorts of spokes in the wheel. Only an enlightened manager would realize that by grooming his second in command he too could progress. In fact, certain managements make it a point to see that a manager makes himself 'surplus' by grooming the second in command. Every opportunity should be given to the bright employee to take up additional responsibilities so that he could continue to accept challenges rather than engage himself in a running battle with the boss who impedes his progress. Unfortunately, such an approach by a manager is an exception than a rule.

Whether one likes it or not an employee is working for himself first then to the organization. That means the employee's likes, dislikes and ambitions might come in the way of that person's commitment to the organization. This is the *What Is It For Me Factor (WIIFM),* which drives an employee while working. That organization, which gives opportunities for the individual to fulfil his personal ambitions, has already won half the battle for the mind of that person. He would, naturally, be loyal to it knowing fully that he is being taken care of and that the management has a keen interest in his progress in the organization. In such cases, he is unlikely to be tempted by offers from other companies.

Take for example, sending an engineer for overseas training. The organization hopes that person would come back and put the training to good use. However, an employee might renege on his promise to return to work. Nevertheless, that is the risk one takes in the larger interest of the company. Taking care of an individual's needs could pay rich dividends in the long-run by way of bonding him to the cause of the organization.

Corporates are searching for catchy slogans that serve to remind the public and consumers at large about their philosophy of doing business. That is also to enhance the brand appeal for the public and consumers at large. In the earlier days, with little competition, corporates were complacent. "Why should we advertise our product as our brand sells by itself?" would be the boastful comment of a CEO who had monopolized the market. Now practically every company, big/medium/small is finding the need to stay in the limelight through advertisements from all possible media. Some are imaginative ads that reflect the corporate philosophy. Others are more to the point telling the public/consumers what sort of products/services they offer.

A few such examples are given in the Table below:

TABLE

"Boldness changes everything" – *ArcelorMittal. Transforming tomorrow*
"Bosch Innovation. Invented for life"– *Bosch*
"Creating wealth not money" – *DSP Merrill Lynch*
"Oberoi hotels prefer to chase quality over quantity" – *Oberoi group of hotels*
"Total integrated automation" – *Siemens*
"Our quality redefines perfection worldwide. Our customers endorse it." – *Crompton Greaves.* Every day solutions
"IDBI Bank – total corporate solutions" – *IDBI Bank*
"One simple philosophy shapes our wealth creations Knowledge First." *Motilal Oswal*
"Our focus is the key to our success" —*Anonymous*

What a Corporate should do

Corporations have to show that they care for the consumers and are not there just to make a profit. They should strive to build a brand image that lasts and creates a favourable impression with the consumers over a period of time. Employees of a corporation should be proud to be part of a famous and ethical company that cares not only for its employees, stakeholders, vendors but also the public at large. Giving priority to 'green' issues is no longer a fad but a necessity. Every company has the onus of reducing greenhouse gases that affect climate change adversely. Pollution laws should be observed in letter and spirit as these are made for the well being of the community at large.

Pollution has crossed national boundaries and a corporation has to think globally about its impact on the environment.

There are a few organizations, which swear by 'green' products and ethical products to attract those who have concern for the environment. *Indian companies have to take more green initiatives to control climate change, which is assuming more and more importance due to global warming.* Organizations will have to learn from each other. The best practices from organizations could be useful for other industries/sectors to be used as benchmark.

A series of disclosures of irregularities, including fudging of accounts, have shattered the public's confidence in companies. One wonders how many more skeletons in the cupboard would tumble out thus making people cynical about the organizations, which until recently they had held them in high esteem. It is clear, once the image is sullied due to any wrongdoing, it would be a Herculean task to regain public confidence. *Ethics in business thus is assuming greater and greater importance, than the bottom-line.*

> The shareholders might excuse a company for making a loss once in a way but can never countenance any unethical practice, which would harm the image of that company.

Ethical products/services: Some companies take pride in the fact they bring out only ethical products/services which enhance the quality of life. On the other hand, the fly-by-night operators, interested in quick profits, would do anything to sell their wares unmindful of any consequences to the users. They might make a tidy profit by selling to the gullible, pack up, and disappear from the scene. A product, which states that it would give relief when taken by, say, an arthritis patient should do so, without ifs and buts.

Ethical practices: Employees are assets treated the right way. However, their loyalty to the company they are working for cannot be taken for granted just because the management is paying a fair wage and compensation. Moreover, stress management for employees must be made mandatory for companies in India. That is more so when the job market has opened up due to competition, which results in stressful life within the working hours and even outside. The hiring procedures should be transparent and there should be no underhand dealings by way of corruption and nepotism in hiring people. The vendors should be treated as part of the team and should get a fair price for their goods/services. A number of goods, like saris, ready-made clothes, are being foisted upon gullible consumers who are attracted by 'seconds', 'export surplus' and the like which give them a price advantage but cannot hope to have any quality guarantee. In such cases the sales clause, 'goods once sold cannot be returned or exchanged', holds good by the very nature of the sale. Customers should be warned there is no guarantee of quality on such dubious sales.

Government regulations: Whether an organization likes it or prepared for it or not, there are certain government regulations in force in a business milieu. Such regulations are designed for the good of the public and so should be adhered to in letter and spirit. Pollution control, for instance, is necessary in these days where the public have become more aware of the impact of pollution on the environment and on their health. A toxic pollutant should be properly treated before discharging into water bodies or underground. So too is the treatment of exhaust gases from factory chimneys, which should meet air quality standards laid down.

> A responsible organization would not hesitate to recall any production batch where they suspect some problem instead of suppressing it or waiting for consumers to complain.

Social responsibility: A business which ignores social and other factors which affect the public is seen in poor light by the shareholders, the employees and the public. It has to take care of the environment in which it is operating. Some organizations have planted trees in and around their place of operation. They employ physically and mentally challenged persons and give them suitable jobs so that they could make a living with dignity. Any civic cause, like beautifying gardens, parks and monuments would receive attention from the organizations in an attempt to be part of the city from which they operate. They would be the first to come out strongly in support of the community in case of any disaster, natural calamities like earthquake, flood or man-made disasters like fire.

It is not enough these days to be profitable from quarter to quarter. *What is more important is the image, which an organization projects to the public.* The public is very sensitive about an organization, which has duped them by adopting unethical practices. Once there is erosion in the public confidence, the future of such an organization is doomed. That is the reason why the top executives are encouraging their employees to follow strictly ethical practices rather than take recourse to illegal and corrupt practices for short-term gains. For that to happen, the CEO and members of the management team have to be walking and talking examples of honesty and ethical practices. Proactive steps to prevent aberrations by employees should receive top priority by the CEO. The recent incident of persons selling confidential information in the BPO industry, leaking defence secrets to foreign countries, and trying to copy designs to beat the competition are some of the illegal and unethical cases that have come to light. *Independent auditors should be watchdogs of an organization for suggesting timely and decisive actions to the top management to nip any illegal activity in the bud.* They should act like eyes and ears for the management of the organization they have been hired to conduct independent audit and offer suggestions for all-round improvement.

The modern corporation is knowledge-based which is keen to hire and retain talent and promote excellence in every field of organizational work.

> There is a sea change in the organizational culture to fall in line with the best practices of others, which serve as benchmark. Already there is a change from fixed hours of working to flexible hours, where possible.

A New Paradigm

Thanks to liberalization and globalization a few organizations in India are compelled to bring out products of International quality. Moreover low cost products of foreign origin are flooding the market. The consumers of today are confronted with a plethora of products of international quality. Thus, the consumer has a 'problem of plenty' on his/her hands. In order to see that the hard earned money is put to good use the consumer has to do home work to stay abreast of the trends. On the other hand the producers have realized that ours is a competitive market and hence mere slogans or glitzy advertisements would not last long to woo consumers who now have a real choice. Some of them had to re-study the market trends to fine-tune their product range to make these visible to consumers. However, what needs a change is in the attitude of the dealers and sales-persons who have to realize ours is no more a sheltered market and dictate terms to consumers who hold the purse strings.

A statement like, "We can supply what we produce, nothing else," is slowly, but surely, changing to, "We shall deliver whatever you want." Such a sea change in attitude is brought about, thanks to the opening up of the markets to domestic as well as overseas suppliers. Instead of taking customers for a ride, it is the clear intention to satisfy them that is spawning a new brand of players well tuned to the competitive market of today. Customers had never had it so good, with producers, suppliers and financiers bending backwards to woo the customers with prompt and polite service. However, a word of caution: we have miles to go before we could reach the standards of the pampered customers of the advanced countries where they are treated as kings.

Flexibility means the producer is trying to satisfy the needs of a customer however big or small he might be. However, a few suppliers believe that not all customers are the same and so they apply the 80-20 rule to distinguish those important customers who form the bulk of their clientele. What counts is the promptness and service with a smile that attracts and retains customers. If a supplier states, "We will deliver the 100 number of pistons you ordered by 15th March, we will do so without fail and without ifs and buts." What is not appreciated is the fact that nowadays, both domestic and overseas customers, place much importance to the deliver commitment without fail. *Lack of delivery commitment is also poor quality*. In fact, if the delivery takes part too early or too late it is just the same and could lead to customer dissatisfaction. Some of our exporters have not understood the reality of exports. They think they could get away with poor quality after getting orders by sending good products at the initial approval stage.

New paradigm: How does one achieve flexibility in operations? By focussing on customers' needs. The operations to satisfy the needs of a customer within an organization have to conform to a degree of standardization so that the operations within its framework could be changed, with minimal efforts, to deliver goods promised. In other words, the process parameters might be different from one product to another but the setting up time is minimized by having trained and skilled personnel who could start and complete the processes within a time-bound frame with ease. That is the reason why standardizing the various operations within the plant is assuming so much importance.

The ability of a producer to deliver a few of a kind makes him a formidable competitor. Though the scale for an economic production could be a large order, the supplier by his skills is able to complete a small order to the satisfaction of the customer. It should be remembered that a satisfied customer is the best sales person for the company. Many a company has failed to see the logic in delivering even small quantity orders, though it might not be all that profitable. It is quite possible that the same customer after satisfying himself that the company is genuinely interested in his orders could raise the quantities in the next order or could keep him as a second supplier for another product he is about to launch. Other consumers too could be attracted to such a customer-friendly company.

In order to deal with such small orders, a separate unit for batch production could be set-up. Costing for a small order could prove tricky. However, a producer who is interested in a customer might not go all out in jacking up the price of a small order to cover his costs. If he does that, he is following the book no doubt but is likely to lose that customer. Nevertheless, a reasonable hike in price is acceptable to the customer knowing that it takes extra efforts to set-up and process a small order. With increased orders, the supplier is likely to gain from the business. The producer is interested in an economical batch quantity from an order by a customer but will make an exception so that it could hope to garner future orders. The willingness to accommodate small orders is the hallmark of good suppliers. Moreover, he has gained the confidence of the customer whose word-of-mouth publicity could trigger more orders from others. On the other hand, a dissatisfied customer could prove to be a hindrance.

Size: A small unit could handle a small order better than a big one.

> The restructuring exercise is a means to make an organization 'lean and mean'.

Some units have opened special designated sub-units for batch production, meant exclusively for small order customers. Top managers set the tone for any flexible approach as an acceptable system when needed to satisfy a customer, however small he might be. Once the senior executives accept flexibility in operations as a way of life, others too, after discussion and counselling, are likely to follow suit. Every member of the team has committed himself to faster delivery despite the size of an order. However, the tendency to pay more attention to a big order from an important customer than a sporadic order from a small customer is but natural.

Flexibility is the mantra for success in these days of intense customer focus. If the management adopts the strategy that it shall not lose any customer because of the size of the order, it has already won half the battle. The tools for executing a small order would have to be adapted suitably and in time. For instance, it might not be difficult for a production shop to change its set-up overnight to execute a small batch production. In fact a few organizations have organized within their unit a 'small batch production' shop as a separate entity, which makes it far easier to cater to the needs of small customers. Another alternative is to 'farm out' to reliable vendors on the basis of 'vendor-on-the-team'. A small order could be easily delivered by the very nature of the small vendor(s) who might get all the technical/financial assistance needed from the bigger unit. "Small order-small vendor" could be the ideal fit. *Ultimately it is the approach and attitude to keep customers happy that counts.*

Are we Really "shining" after Liberalization and Globalization?

A sheltered market, closed economy model, shut out all competition from outside. Our government believed in the theory that Indian customers were happy with whatever was produced within the country. That was the way to encourage '*Swabhiman*' which meant self-respect. It was a demonstration to the world that we could manage our economy independently. Winds of change blew in and we had to open our windows to the outside world believing it would help us and more importantly our competitive edge in the overseas market would improve when we allow liberal imports. We have seen how the customs duty on several products has been slashed and the process is continuing. Gone are the days when a consumer had to wait long for his/her goods/services. In a few product sectors imports have no doubt hit our domestic producers hard who have no option but to improve their efficiency and slash down their prices too so that these could compete with the foreign brands. There are a few organizations, which claim, justifiably—"At the centre of India's markets. At the leading edge."—Best Investment Bank—India. "A passion to perform"—Deutsche Bank.

Paeans are sung on the reforms that have opened the Indian market to competition—domestic as well as foreign. From a market where one had to wait for years for one's favourite goods, with poor quality thrown in, we have now the luxury of multi-choice with goods and services meeting international quality. The haves are rubbing their hands in glee as they could afford to buy top quality goods without leaving our shores. It is history when every passenger arriving from overseas used to carry a two-in, TV, microwave oven, food processor or some such stuff, often to be sold in a captive market at handsome profits. *But when it comes to the choice and availability of basic goods and services there is a lot to be desired.* It looks as though the underprivileged have missed the bus once again. They have still to contend with poor quality stuff dished out by the fair price shops, wait in long lines for a meager quota of kerosene and struggle to get their daily water standing in lines at the public taps and get squeezed in overcrowded trains and buses. The life of the common man has improved marginally, if at all.

> Bottom line is the mantra driving the domestic and foreign enterprises that have to cope with tough competition.

Each one is vying with the other in getting the attention of the consumers who sometimes turn choosy. Tall talk or freebies do not sway them. They often demand and get value for their hard earned money. As per the well-known *Pareto* principle in economics just twenty per cent of the population has almost eighty per cent of the buying power.

> The rise of the middle class in our country is truly phenomenal. This class has so many numbers that it is more than the population of several countries put together which makes sense to the Indian and foreign companies to attract this clientele.

Goods and services are targeted keeping in mind the middle class and the upper class society who have the purchasing power. It is a fact that in several cities the luxury car like the Mercedes Benz and the Rolls Royce, the highest symbol of luxury and class, costing crores of rupees has buyers.

The process of liberalisation and globalisation is expected to have increased the growth rate (to about 9 per cent) and benefited one and all. The argument goes, for example, with one car sold, many, about twenty people, are benefited—right from the sales outlet, service set-up, and petrol pumps to the domestic help who cleans the car daily. That trickle down effect is what is being hailed as positive fallout of the process of economic reforms, apart from the availability of goods and services, mostly, catering to those who have the purchasing power. That's why statistics released now and then point out to the reduction in the number of those below the poverty line, though by way of sheer numbers they still account for millions. Just like in those nations who have embraced economic reforms by way of abandoning state control and central planning, we too are suffering the ill-effects of the reforms that have harmed a section of the population instead of helping them.

The flip side: Jobs are shrinking and unemployment is increasing due to stiff competition which has put a brake on employment and the need to make the organization lean and less top heavy. VRS, the so-called "golden handshake" has attempted to get rid of excess staff. But in that process, some good people have left the organization affecting the quality of service offered by them, for example, Banks are forced to work with less people. With diminishing returns, those who thought that the lump sum offered by the organizations would keep them happy are in trouble. Moreover, rarely, they get the lump sum but only bonds and other financial instruments that could be enjoyed only after a few years. With not much job opportunities, those who have opted for VRS are a disappointed lot. They are prepared for any job so that they can earn a bit and keep themselves occupied rather than sit at home and idle. The lure of VRS is diminishing rapidly. However, for those who would unlearn and learn new trades are in demand as some of the areas in the economy are showing big growths like in communication, entertainment, health care, hospitality, tourism and transport.

As far as choice for the underprivileged in those items they could afford to buy, they have little to cheer about. The PDS now meant for only the Below Poverty Line (BPL) families has become a joke with no one interested in improving the quality of the stuff sold. For the middle class, the ration card now serves as an identity card only. However, such a luxury of not purchasing from the PDS outlets is not there for the poor and the needy that depend almost entirely on the PDS outlets meant to supply cheap and good stuff. There is no powerful lobby that could work to improve the quality of food grains supplied by the PDS. The poor have nowhere to go to complain and, moreover, they have little time or enthusiasm to do so. Thus it's a stoic acceptance of their fate to eat substandard food grains and long waits for a meager quota.

> Big business is mostly interested in big bucks only and not so socially committed to improve the lot of the underprivileged. There are fortunately exceptions to this general rule.

If the government itself has abandoned these people, it's too much to expect the profit motivated private organizations to help. So economic reform for such people has not much meaning. The world may be 'flat' for the technical savvy and the haves, but for the have-nots the world is very much 'round', which has no sympathy for their lot. It looks as though capitalism is slowly but surely becoming fashionable with few takers for socialism. However, the reality is there are many children of smaller gods who are crying for attention and care. The clarion call of the Prime Minister while addressing business tycoons that they should spare a thought for the underprivileged has not come a day too late. We need socially committed, community-oriented, environmentally friendly businesses to flourish while caring for the have-nots. We need an 'all-inclusive' growth, however Utopian it might sound.

CORPORATES AND COMMUNITY DEVELOPMENT

That corporate houses are taking active part in the community development is welcome news. *Businesses have realized that it's not enough to show a healthy bottom-line but they must offer something more to the social and community development of which they are part and parcel.* Some have confined themselves to beautifying their environment by having plush and green lawns and green trees all around in their factories and offices while others have been doing yeoman service to the upliftment of the community by various welfare measures benefiting the masses. Such enlightened interest in the community benefits not only the community but also the image of the corporation, which is doing exemplary service besides running a profitable ethical business.

> By taking part in community service an organization shows its 'human face' that would enhance its corporate image.

Contrast this with the attitude of another company, which does not show any interest in the welfare of the community it is part of. Not surprisingly, people in the community would have a low opinion about such a company, which appears too commercial bereft of any feeling or concern for the community but for its profitability only.

As a good example how corporates perform their self-imposed task of community welfare measures, it is interesting to get a peep into the community development activities undertaken by the giant Reliance Industries Ltd. That industry has focussed on healthcare, education, child welfare, and village infrastructure development.

Reliance serves not only its employees but also offers medical facilities to people in and around the plant. Nearby communities are served by the hospitals at Reliance plant and also through mobile vans carrying the required medical equipments and trained staff. The emphasis is on providing health care to the children through vaccination and pulse polio camps. The company also organizes regular health check-ups to schoolchildren in the community. Awareness of family planning and blood donation too forms part of the health drive. In a year over 1200 patients are treated in eye-camps organized through the Lion's Club at the Reliance Patalganga plant. Mobile dispensary unit provides health-related service to the villagers at their Hazira complex. Blood donation camps are a regular feature of the efforts to get blood donated voluntarily.

The stress is on providing high quality education for all the employee's, children as well as the nearby villagers. These schools have the modern infrastructure—library, laboratory and computers. The children have access to good playing fields and sports facilities too. Reliance also provides support to nearby schools by providing assistance to building schools, providing computers and sports equipments. Inter-schools competitions in athletics, singing, essay writing and sports such as volleyball, tennis and cricket are organized regularly with support from Reliance.

The company provided 8 million gallons of drinking water to Jam Khambhalia village during the summer of 2003 when there was an acute water shortage. It also built a drinking water storage sump of 20-lakh-litre capacity near the railway station in record time to enable rail water tankers to provide water to the nearby villages. Water was also provided through road water tankers to a few villages near the Reliance complex at Moti Khavdi. Assistance was offered to repair water pumps and lay water pipes to villages. Reliance Rural Development Trust (RRDT) is helping the Gujarat government in improving the village infrastructure through building community hall, anganwadis, panchayats offices and improving village roads.

The above is just one example how a giant corporate business has involved in community development. However, that is by no means unique. *Several other companies, both big and small, do help in community development activities in various fields that improve the quality of life of the people*. Such involvement is likely to increase given the corporates' desire to gain the goodwill of the people, which is a good business strategy too. In fact, such work increases the esteem of a business house in the eyes of the public.

CHALLENGES OF THE CYBER-AGE

The advent of the cyber-age is real in a vast country like ours. Who could have imagined the connectivity in this large geographically underdeveloped nation would be so good and be the envy of even some of the developed nations. There is a furious pace to spread the use of mobile phones, which has become a common gadget used by the lowest members of the social strata. Being computer savvy is taken for granted. Those who were once used to the typewriters have willingly accepted use of computers.

The Cyber-age is on—whether we like it or prepared for it or not. Typewriters are being junked and typists are entering the endangered species list. Now every office, worth its name, has computers. Paperless offices are the trend. Huge registers collecting dust might be outdated even in government and semi-government offices. Bank customers might have to wait for attention at the counters where the employees are busy looking at the computer screen and typing away furiously on the keyboard. Almost all railway stations in the country have computerized reservation offices. So, what does these mean to citizens in the country some of whom are suffering from a fear complex of the cyber-age? They were more comfortable with people and registers and personalized service at a leisurely pace. Now everyone is busy, in offices or even in homes, working on computers. Cash-issuing clerks are being replaced by smart ATMs.

> The fact is the cyber-age is on—the hope that it would go away as a fad is misplaced.

Unless everyone is prepared to handle the cyber-age in a proper manner, he would have the same fate as the dinosaurs. Some of the middle-aged and older persons who think that the cyber-age is of no use to them are facing a bleak future. In offices, computer literacy is necessary and now all recruitments at most of the places are based, besides other requirements, on the candidates' proficiency in computers. That explains why IT education is receiving more attention. Even small children attend some of these classes, as summer courses. Good educational institutions have set-up their own computer laboratories where teachers and students are trained to use them for educational purposes. Some of the software packages are targeted towards enhancing learning skills. Class assignments, tests and examinations are being done through computers.

Those who want to enter the job market have a tough time now with the market for jobs shrinking in every sector. The IT balloon has almost burst dashing the hopes of millions of job-seekers, with the recession in the US market (2007-08) being one of the major reasons for the slow down. Many young men and women who opted for IT industry are in trouble. They find that even big IT companies are paring their staff strength and new recruitments are put on hold. That was bound to happen eventually given the fact that IT industry is a service industry and does not manufacture consumer products. Its application might be across the board but still it has its limitation for adoption. The more sophisticated the IT package, like the ERP solutions, the more complicated and expensive these would be to buy and train the people. Faced with a cash crunch, some of the prospective industries have opted for smaller software packages or postponed their introduction for the future hoping for an upturn in the recessionary market of the present. A lot of sectors of late (2008) have a problem of availability of skilled personnel. That cannot be solved by increasing wages and salaries but addressing to the basic problem of short supply by increasing availability of skilled persons in various disciplines.

The ordinary person who might not be directly into the IT business has to cope with the burgeoning use of computers practically in every walk of life. For instance, PCs have made deep inroads into Indian homes. Thanks to the E Mail, Cyber Chat and others, very few consumers would like to be left behind in using computers for their daily needs. With the click of a mouse, he could access any airline schedule and book a ticket for himself. If one knows the PNR number one could find out one's rail reservation status in seconds instead of phoning lines, which are always busy or commute long distance to the railway reservation counters. With the Internet Banking, a customer has a choice—not to go to the bank but carry out all the transactions—credit, debit, status of account *et. al.* from the comfort of one's own home. Gone are the days where one had to issue cheques and stand in a line to pay electricity, water, and telephone bills. Banking through the electronic way, like the ECS, has saved much of the hassles. For some customers, such a change is too drastic and they would need more time mentally to get used to the 'paper-less' way.

A line in caution, however, is useful. *Computers do not make mistakes but people do!* So it is always better to check whether a certain transaction has taken place on time and correctly. Crediting a wrong account in a bank transaction might be rare but still goes on. Then there are the credit/debit card frauds which are one of the biggest frauds going on. That is why one has to be careful about such transactions where direct interface might not be there. A blind trust in the system has to be replaced with a certain degree of caution as we might be dealing with a few persons who may be inefficient, crooked or corrupt. However, such freak mishaps should not deter a person going the electronic way. For example, credit/debit cards are a boon to the consumers replacing bank notes with a plastic card. For sheer convenience, nothing could beat these.

> The advantages of the cyber-age far outweigh the lacunae, largely man-made, and deserve careful consideration even by those conservative persons who are happy purchasing with crisp notes and who are comfortable looking at human faces. Those who are keen to be in step with the cyber-age should put in self-study or attend IT courses to become computer literate at least.

RATING

Companies/organizations are being rated every year by Business Magazines to help investors to determine the company/organization which they could trust/invest. Such rating could change from year to year and so one has to keep in touch with the latest survey to benefit from such an independent appraisal/rating of a company/organization. Various parameters are chosen carefully so that the rating is made realistic. A few organizations show outstanding performance as far as HRD is concerned. Others give special attention to training/orientation to make the employees up-to-date in their skills. Compensation/benefit package is another interesting criterion which has been given special attention to attract talent and retain them. There are a few organizations/companies which give intense attention to the important aspect of recruitment. *These and more aspects could be studied by going through the rating of each company, which has made the list by a reputed Business Magazine from year to year.*

Here is an example how the *best companies to work for in India* are rated [Reference: *Business Today*, November 15, 2007]

1. Microsoft India (Ranking 1 in 2007). [Note: all rankings for 2007]
   Microsoft secret sauce:
   - Leadership development
   - Internal transfers
   - Transparent compensation
   - Mentoring
   - Recruitment
2. Infosys Technologies (Ranking 5)
   Problems:
   - Growing scale
   - Slow in communication
   - MNC competitors
   - HR lag
   - Slow promotions
   - Attrition is not a major problem
   - Infosys invests heavily on training
3. iGATE (Ranking 6):
   - More opportunities

- Reward system
- Easy access to top management
- Exposure to multiple clients
- Innovation
- Early responsibility

4. Accenture (Ranking 9):
   - Global opportunities
   - Reward system
   - Education initiatives
   - (Online courses for employees with association with MIT etc. to upgrade skills)
   - Career mobility
   - Empowered employees (Even though it is a global giant, Accenture allows employees to take autonomous decisions and gives them budgets to manage them.)
5. Marriott Hotels India (Ranking 11):
   - Two-way communication
   - Employee benefit initiatives (six days off in a month, financial support for higher education, every employee on his/her birthday can stay in the hotel for one day with his/her spouse or family and can dine anywhere)
   - Knowledge initiatives (every Marriott Hotel has a learning centre that has a collection of books and videos, along with an Internet connection)
   - Defined span-of-leadership (There is a Leadership Performance Process Management System which defines nine competencies which a Marriott associate should have to develop)
   - Reward system (There are two kinds of awards for individuals or groups to recognize outstanding performance. Each Marriott Hotel in India has its own awards. This is apart from an overall event involving all Marriott Properties globally)
6. HCL Infosystems (Ranking 13):
   - Rewarding the best is the best way to retain employees
   - Innovation is encouraged
   - Learn from leaders
   - 360-degree feedback (Employees look at aspects of the managers' performance; strategic vision, ability to communicate, problem-solving skills, responsiveness. The results of survey (the ranking and comments) are then aggregated and published Online for everyone to see
   - Employee-management interface
   - Focus on learning
   - Innovation
   - Business continuity plan

- Employee engagement (Some of the new initiatives include MyPal, Three Cheers, Wellness Programme, Little Mindian and Bring a Smile Programme while some of the existing ones are preventive health check-ups, yoga classes, and employee relief fund.

7. Godrej Consumer (Ranking 14):
   - Consumer-orientation
   - Young professional matter
   - HR management system
   - Out-of-the-box programmes
   - Stress on communication
   - Health check-ups
   - Hand in hand employee growth and company growth.
8. Honeyweel Technology Solutions Lab (Ranking 15):
   - Two-way communication (regular meetings by MD and individual business unit leaders with employees to communicate policies and address grievances and operational issues).
   - Employee benefit initiatives (Counselling by health and finance experts. Encourage employees and their families to develop friendship and organize sports and social events).
   - Knowledge initiatives (tie-ups with leading educational institutions like IIMs, IITs, BITS Pilani, Illinois Institute of Technology, Chicago and others for advanced courses for employees that it partially sponsors.
   - Defined span-of-leadership: It has a structured initiative in place to ensure that adequate attention is given to every employee's individual needs.

     Reward system: Employees are categorized into Star Performers and Valued Contributors and achievers are rewarded in an open and transparent manner.
   - Attrition is not a major problem.
9. Mind Tree Consulting (Ranking 2):
   - Empower employees and care for them.
   - Attrition rate of senior managers just1 per cent.
   - Young company and opportunities for people to grow.
10. Johnson and Johnson (Ranking 3):
    - Strong emotional connect with the company.
    - Involvement in community work.
11. Sapient (Ranking 4):
    - Very open and very fair.
    - Transparency.
    - Unique work culture.
    - Great options for career growth.
    - Flexible hours.
12. Agilent Technologies (Ranking 7):

- Leaders spend about 80 per cent of their time in coaching, developing, innovating employees. 20 per cent managing their work.
- Learn and grow.
- Give the people the right tools.
- Support employees to work from home.

13. HCL Comnet (Ranking 8):
    - Innovative HR practices.
    - Focus on people's processes and development.
    - Structured job rotation.
    - Empower employees.
    - Recognition led incentive schemes.
14. Dr Reddy's Labs (Ranking 10):
    - Nurturing global leaders.
    - Change managers get a thumbs up.
    - Promising young leaders are invited to share their breakthrough ideas before the management council at its quarterly meeting.

The Table below indicates the secrets of the Best Managed companies.

TABLE

"10 mantras" of management success:

- Be audacious in your vision
- Focus on what you know best
- Trim flab to achieve operational excellence
- Good governance makes business sense
- Develop leaders from within
- Forge stronger partnerships with your supplier base
- Pursue quality with zeal
- Innovate to create value for customers
- Give back to the society
- The Indian edge

—Tips from Business Today, March 23, 2008

10

Corporates and Culture

—How others see you

"We care for our people" is one of the mottos of a company like the giant IBM Corporation. People are treated as assets and not as liabilities with details of how much each employee costs to hire and maintain. Such an attitude and corporate philosophy starts at the top—the CEO of the organization who sets the tone for business. Every CEO is charged with making profits but the details of how that could be achieved are best left to the CEO who is in charge of directing the operations. That is easier said than done when it comes to carrying on such a philosophy despite the vagaries of business and stiff competition. What does an 'employee-oriented company' do when faced by dwindling sales and going into the red every quarter? After all the CEO has to maintain the financial health of the company despite all external and internal factors. "The buck stops here," is what a CEO has to say rather than find scapegoats among his/her employees.

> The culture in an organization is a complex issue built over a period of time through chairmen and chief executives who give directions to the organization's present and future.

The trend is to continue some of the good practices, be it any field that gives the organization a brand name in the market. *Some organizations pride themselves as being employee-friendly*. That means right from the top to the bottom there is camaraderie that creates a pleasant and conducive environment to work. Keeping the workplace friendly means the boss in charge is careful how he/she deals with his/her people. However, it does not mean there is a laisser-faire approach to people's behaviour. Discipline has to be maintained in any organization for smooth and orderly functioning. There should be a clear understanding what is the *Laxman-Rekha* for conduct under various conditions. If there is a general unrest due to labour union's demands, no one expects normal working conditions to be present all the time. However, a responsible union would instruct its members to behave themselves in a manner that does not cause harm to the superiors, the workplace and the machines. Sabotage is definitely out, as the people will have to resume work in the same place after normalcy is restored. You cannot cut your nose to spite your face, as that would be foolish.

A problem often faced by any organization is whether the top managers like it or accept it or not, there are cliques (groups) that work within the organization to promote their own interests. These are of course, informal but very powerful ones at that. *That kind of groupism is bad for the culture of the organization, which is trying to put up a united front*. The fact is 'birds of a similar feather gather together' and that cannot be helped even among human beings. For instance, those employees working in the R & D department feel superior and think they are the brainy type while those in the production and other departments merely carry on what they have designed and developed. On the other hand, even those working in the packing and transport department are equally smug and proud of their work, however lowly it might appear to the R & D people. "Let us have a fine design and great manufacture. In reality without our excellent packing, handling and transport everything would be ruined. So we too are very important in the customer-satisfaction chain." How true! However, a new entrant would be puzzled at the type of groupism and wonders why he/she cannot be a member of that group straightaway. It is not so simple as that as like in any club there has to be a consensus among the members that the new entrant deserves to be taken on board.

It is a long and hard battle to dismantle these cliques, which stand in the way of integration and oneness of purpose among every employee. However, the CEO could initiate measures that would discourage these groups by informing the managers that he/she does not appreciate these cliques in the interest of teamwork and overall understanding. Those who still pursue their objectives could be warned and as a punitive measure give a lower increment since such managers have failed to integrate well with the rest of the team members. Such firm actions are expected to show results.

CASE STUDY

Let us take an example of how an employee who reports back to work after a long illness is treated. In most companies the immediate boss and sometimes his/her boss too would have already visited the sick employee to find out how that employee was getting on. All the help that's possible, including finance where it's provided would have been offered to the employee to see that he/she got well. In a people-oriented set-up, the concerned manager is all-solicitous to see that the employee is comfortable and that he/she takes matters easy for the first few days at least. He/she is caring for the employee's well-being and is ready to give him/her lighter work initially. Moreover, any request for leaving the organization early or additional leave of absence is readily agreed upon by the understanding boss who is trained and motivated by the higher-ups to keep the employee's interest at heart as far as possible in taking decisions.

Contrast with another organization where people are mere cogs in the wheel of production and delivery, which come first. The boss would confront the employee after reporting for duty after a long leave of absence due to sickness. No manager or any representative of the management would have visited the ailing employee, as it's 'none of our business'. However, some organizations do send the manager concerned just to make sure the ailment is 'genuine' and not an excuse to stay away from work or utilize the generous sick leave of the company by moonlighting or simply lazing around at the company's cost. There is mutual suspicion between such a management set-up and the employees where trust is lacking.

> Cultural issues are a part of the complexities of doing business across borders, this being the age of globalization with acquisitions, consolidation, mergers, takeovers and buyouts.

Manageability of workforce and other HR issues are important considerations while making a decision to set-up foreign operations. Integrating global companies for meeting the common goal of the corporation is a great experience (challenge) and helps to bring in more diversity into the organization. "The collaborative nature of work across the globe and technologies have made unlearning more relevant in today's context. What works for one culture might not work for another,"—says an International management expert. That is the reason why a manager who is posted abroad has to unlearn the culture he/she is so used to. On the other hand, every effort should be made to understand and appreciate the culture of the people he/she would be dealing with. The manager should have an open mind and be receptive to an alien culture. It would help matters if the senior manager(s) learn at least a smattering of the local language where they need to operate.

CASE STUDY

A young dynamic American manager was posted to an American owned Japanese company operating in Japan as the general manager. He was keen to implement the suggestion box scheme which he had heard so much that gave many suggestions for saving costs and also quality/productivity improvement. He announced that individuals would be awarded handsome cash/gifts for acceptable suggestions that helped the organization. He did consult his managers who endorsed the idea though some of them had doubts about its success. The scheme was introduced with a big bang and the general manager was keenly awaiting suggestions to pour in. He had already planned a big function to celebrate the award of the first accepted suggestion. The suggestion boxes were set-up at various places in the factory premises, shop floor and including the canteen, library and recreation center.

He requested his Japanese colleagues, after one week, to go around and find out how many suggestions had poured in at the various centers. The Japanese returned with a morose face and blurted out, "Sir, I am sorry. There has been no suggestion at all in any box." The American was stunned to hear such admission of total failure. He was highly disturbed and called a meeting of his senior managers that very evening and requested them to be frank and tell him what had gone wrong. One of the Japanese managers stood up and explained why the scheme had failed to enthuse the people. The underlining factor of the present suggestion box scheme was the premise that individuals would be rewarded, which was against the Japanese culture of teamwork. "How can the management single out a person for reward when the team had done a good job?" asked another manager who knew his people well. The American boss lost no time in modifying the suggestion box scheme that emphasized the fact that winning teams would be selected for accepted suggestions rather than individuals and all the team members would get equal share of the reward in cash/ kind. That saw a sea change in the attitude of the workers and suggestions poured in soon afterwards.

> There are a few organizations whose reputation for handling their employees leaves much to be desired.

CASE STUDY

An organization in Pune, a medium size one, was notorious for its ham-handed approach to its employees. Employees were treated curtly and without any consideration for their feelings. One story that went around the corporate world was that of a senior manager of that company who had gone abroad on an assignment. There was difference of opinion between him and the CEO who lost no time in giving that manager the marching orders. How that was done was shocking. The CEO sent his personal secretary to the airport to meet the senior manager. He was given the sack order signed by the CEO. A cheque in lieu of full settlement due to him was handed over by the personal secretary right at the exit of the airport terminal. His official car was withdrawn at the airport itself and he had to engage a private taxi to return home. One cannot imagine a worse treatment than this, which was so insensitive and humiliating and that too meted to a senior manager who had served the company so well for many years. That such inhuman form of 'culture' still prevails in a few organizations is shocking. In these organizations people are treated as dirt and without an iota of sensitivity. That shocking piece of news reached the Chairman of the Board of Directors a bit late. He was furious with such a drastic step, which had brought ridicule to the entire organization. He warned all his CEOs not to indulge in petty behaviour and show off their might. "You have to be more sensitive to people," he advised them. But he had to uphold the decision of his subordinate though with great reluctance.

The business practices, including HR practices, are changing fast to meet the challenges of globalization. Managing attrition is still a big challenge to corporations, which are trying their best to keep the attrition rate, due to various internal as well as external factors, within limits. *Managing growth in the regime of acquisitions, mergers and closures is not easy.* The HR functions have to be dynamic to understand the complexities. Managing a heterogeneous workforce is a challenge and an opportunity to an organization. Leadership development and managing a 'virtual team' is interesting. There are now more opportunities for organizations to learn from each other using their best practices, modified to suit an organization. Compensation package to be offered to the CEO, directors and senior managers is an on-going exercise and have to be affordable as well as innovative to attract the best talent and retain them. Often such a compensation package is decided by the industry norm as well as one's own paying capacity. Training and motivational methods have to be adapted to each organization but one could gain from the failure as well as success of others.

Symbols of Culture

"We care for our people", "We care for the environment we operate", "We value our stakeholders", "Vendors on our team", such statements indicate the corporate culture of a few companies who want to proclaim their commitment to various aspects of running a business. The only problem arises when, despite such statements, some one somewhere adopts devious methods and spoils the name of the company. "The buck stops here," the CEO would say and he/she is responsible for whatever that happens within and outside the organization. *To maintain high standards is difficult but that is how a company gets a brand name and a reputation in the market*. The above are just a few symbols of culture of the organization that is often visible to the public. Mr. Philips one time the chairman of the giant corporation N.V. Philips based in The Netherlands was a fountainhead of compassion for the people working in the organization. He used to lecture about his commitment to building bridges of understanding with his people by setting a personal example of greeting his secretary every day and especially after the weekend how he/she spent the vacation. He exhorted in his talks and discussions that in the MNC's overseas organizations a philosophy of personal touch should be preached and practiced.

Professional Culture

> A few organizations take pride in fostering excellence.

For example, Harvard Business School prides itself for being the unchallenged school for business due to its high standard and rigorous selection procedure. That applies to some companies who want nothing but the best by offering attractive salaries, perks, overseas training and other incentives, which are hard to refuse by young persons. R & D organizations, be it IBM, Ford, GM, Infosys, put a high premium on highly qualified persons to conduct research and development that could have a far reaching impact on the fortune of the company. Everyone tries to be the first to introduce a new product that would have a head start before competitors try to catch up. For that to happen the companies need highly talented dedicated professionals who continue to reinvent themselves by focusing on improving their qualifications. Companies take pride in the fact that they have some of the best persons on their rolls, a boost for the company's brand image. Innovation is the keyword when it comes to development.

> Organizations desire to have qualified persons for the simple reason they want to get the best out of them for getting outstanding business results.

However, people are given full freedom to carry on research and the professionals expect development free from interference from the higher-ups once the main objective of the organization is clear. They are aware they need to produce not only research papers, apply for patents and enjoy freedom to work but they should also bring out products that improve the quality of life of millions of consumers. By such work, the company too gets the benefit by way of increased sales, leading to a healthy bottom line. *Continuing education/certification have assumed greater importance in view of rapid changes*. Apart from company-sponsored programmes, the individual is encouraged to take up courses that enhance that person's skills. There are part-time courses, evening courses and on-line courses that a person could take up to improve skills and stay up-to-date. The company offers to reimburse expenses incurred by such activity by individuals. That is way of promoting professionalism in the organization.

CULTURE OF RECOGNITION

An important aspect of a management is that of recognizing talent and achievement. Organizations have various ways of recognizing achievements. These include—promotions, awards, rewards, certificate of merit, cash/kind bonus, treat for the family/paid vacations, write-up about the achiever in the company's magazine, arranging a big meeting where outstanding achievers are awarded letters of appreciation/prize/cash and so on. Even a simple letter of appreciation from the manager in-charge could motivate an employee. Peer recognition is another way of applauding the achievement of a colleague. In some cases, big photographs of the 'outstanding person of the month' are displayed giving details of the person's achievement. Sometimes even a simple pat on the back of the achiever by the boss is considered a way of recognizing that person's contribution to the improvement in quality/productivity/safety/saving.

Here are a few advertisements by Corporates/Companies/ Organizations that reflect their culture and concern:

"Because you're special"—Skoda auto for their car *Fabia*
"Delighting our toughest customers"—Sarovar Hotels & Resorts
"Submit Your Dreams to Nature"—Presiidency Group. Township Promoters
"The Complete Man"—Raymond since 1925
"Whatever your taste, we've got it covered"—GRT Hotels & Resorts. *The promise of more*
"Re-live the tradition"—Navrathan Jewellers

"Colours of India come alive"—SONY Television for their brand *Bravia*
"Japan's NO.1 Engine oil now in India"—Nippon Oil Company for *Eneos* brand oil
"Colours work because they talk to the heart"—Ricoh for colour printer
"Switch to the breakfast that scores 7/7"—Nestle's *Cerevita* cereal
"Where do we look when there are no fossil fuels to look for"—Suzlon for wind power
"How to prevent the invasion of rain, wind, noise, dust and pollution" —*Windows do wonders, Fenesta,* Window and Door Systems
"You want only the BEST for your vehicle. Why should the fuel by any different?" Indian Oil for *Xtra Premium* for petrol with friction free buster and *Xtra Mile* for Super Diesel.
"Invented for life"—Bosch
"Turning the wheels of industries, Worldwide"—Shanti Gears Limited
"Sleep like you stand"—Kurl-on Spring Mattress
"World-class roof tiles from the world leader in roofing systems"—MONIER Roofing. *Roofs for living*
"New dimensions in tiling and bath solutions"—Studio Atlas Concorde
"Classic choice for chairpersons"—*pan*—Office Systems Pvt. Ltd.
"Miracles happen in 7 days"—Pond's *age miracle*
"Things that make your home special"—Home Town
"My brother is the world's best all-rounder!"—*brother*®, Brother International Corp., Japan
"Want to colour away the years? Now you can..."—L'OREAL Paris. *Because you are worth it*

"Enhance retention of *skin proteins* with the gentle and effective care of *Fiama Di Wills Skinsense* soap"—ITC Limited

"Bathtubs, cubicles, showers/panels, sanitaryware, fittings pumps. Surprisingly priceless"—Milano ®. *You deserve it*

"Is your family living with germs?" Lizol 3-in-1. *Recommended by Indian Medical Association*

"It follows the 'unlikes attract' rule"—Jaguar. *Too good to resist*

"Quality fuels and quality time. Now under one roof"—Club HP

"When you've worked with India in the past, you're better equipped to be a partner in the future"—BAE Systems, Land Systems Company

"Our solutions exceed every expectation. Just anywhere in the world"—Crompton Greaves—*Everyday Solutions*

"Gift delivered to Mumbai 10:30 am, Birthday. On schedule"—First Flight Couriers Ltd.

"We make sense out of shifting"—Agarwal Packers & Movers

"Cargo solutions for the world"—Emirates Skycargo.

"Whatever your business needs, we have a solution"—BSNL, *Connecting India*

"Spreading the magic of Chemistry"—BASF. *The Chemical Company*

"Listening works wonders. Here's proof"—Amway. *We're listening*

"Take a friend to the movies. Compliments of VISA"—VISA

"I'm empowered to be with you, right through" - HDFC Loans

"One for everyone. *Parivar* Mediclaim. A single policy for the entire family"—National Insurance

"Sundarm BNP Paribas *Tax Saver*"—Sundaram BNP Paribas Mutual. *Unearthing opportunities*

"At KVB any city is your city"—Karur Vysya Bank. *Smart way to bank.*

"When safety is first, you last"—United India Insurance Company Ltd. *Solutions that bring back smiles...real fast*

"Home to people the world over"—Brigade Homestead

"For those who aspire to stay ahead, above and away from the crowd"—Rashi *Splendour*, Rashi Developers

"Head to the coast with us"—Goldfinch. *The finest Boutique Hotel*

"Our smallest hearing aid is almost invisible. Advanced technology makes this possible"—GN Resound. *Technology leaders in hearing healthcare worldwide..*

"Why dream of a home when there is a kingdom awaiting for you?" Mahaveer *Kings's Place*

"Towards a better life"—ICICI Bank

"When it comes to *health insurance* I trust only LIC"—Presenting LIC's *Health Plus*

"Easy access any time"—Union Bank of India

"The happiest family holidays"—Club Mahindra Holidays. *Fun, family, forever*

"Reclaim your favourite place in the class" - *Virgin* atlantic

"Nothing can be more relaxing than re-assurance"—Bank of India.

Relationships beyond banking
"It brings a smile on our face, to see one on yours"—PVR Cinemas. *Bringing Smiles*
"When you stay at a comfortable place, work doesn't feel like work"—Palms Hotel
"Some numbers are clues. Some change lives"—24 hour National Helpline. Child Line 1098 Night & Day. *Donate for children in distress*
"Karnataka—One state. Many worlds"—Karnataka Department of Tourism
"Rajasthan. The Incredible state of India"—Rajasthan Tourism

The above are just a few examples to show how a company/organization/corporate wants to advertise its brand name, its concern for consumers and social/community commitment/responsibility.

ENVIRONMENTAL CONCERNS

Indian companies are taking green initiatives to control climate change. Global warming is true, whether one likes it or accepts it or not. Some have planted trees in their factory premises that greens the area providing shade, fresh air and nests for birds. Some of them have undertaken social forestry to promote sustainable development of forests that are used in papermaking.

> Saving energy is a big concern as the energy bill is mounting every year in view of rising costs of crude oil.

Energy efficient machinery is replacing outdated equipments that waste energy. Incandescent lamps are giving place to CFL lamps, as these are energy efficient. The latest technology is being used to upgrade fuel efficiency throughout the units. Pollution control is another aspect that is receiving better attention as the pollution control boards are exercising their authority to penalize those units, which do not adhere to pollution standards for air and water quality. Fines are imposed on polluting units and in extreme cases ordered to close down the offending unit. *A few instances of the CEOs being imprisoned for not adhering to polluting standards are there.* Extracting underground water is a matter of concern by the community as that deprives them of water in the neighbourhood of these factories, which guzzle water at the cost of the people. Cases have come to the notice of the government and also the judiciary where some factories are exploiting labour as well as resources. Such units are given hefty fines to compensate for the havoc caused to the people as well as the environment.

Business Climate and Ethics

It is no doubt a fiercely competitive business world. However, no one is allowed to get away with unethical practices. The recent case where a competitor was alleged to have access to a rival's design details in the F-1 motor car racing disqualified that company for indulging in unethical conduct beside imposing a hefty fine. That is also happening to numerous anti-trust laws where the guilty is levied fines in millions of dollars. Intellectual Property Right (IPR) is assuming greater importance and any infringement in copyright/patent law is taken as a fit case for punishment. Pirated versions of CDs, DVDs, Books, films are going on clandestinely and the original company that has invested much money is the loser. That is the reason why ethics in business, both in the organized as well as unorganized sector is assuming greater importance than before due to liberalization and globalization. An introduction to spiritualism to one and all could make a big difference to the attitude of the people, at all levels, in this materialistic world where dog eats dog.

ORGANIZATIONAL BEHAVIOUR

> Consistency in the behaviour of an organization is what the employee, union, stakeholder, vendor and general public expects from a reputed organization.

For instance, the management of such a company would behave responsibly towards their recognized union(s). It will not do anything to browbeat the union or try to break the unity by resorting to unethical means.

As far as vendors are concerned, fair pricing should be adopted and not try to squeeze the last rupees from them as they are dependent upon the big organization to survive. That is why some enlightened organizations adopt a policy of 'vendor-on-the-team" which means the vendor is treated as if it is part of the organization, though with a separate identity. No investment is spared to bring the vendor to the standard level of quality, productivity and efficiency. Experts are sent to the vendor(s) site to give on-the-spot assistance when requested. Regular vendor contacts are established to smoothen business relations.

The attitude of a management towards its employees determines the working relationship between the company and its employees. Some resort to short-cut methods to make a profit.

Case Study

A small manufacturing company in Pune used to take graduate apprentices who were asked to work like workers in shifts on a pittance of an allowance. Some of them resented such a 'training' schedule and left. In fact, that suited the company, which went on taking fresh graduates to make up the workforce. That was done under the guise of giving the trainees work experience but actually they were production workers. It was production work that the apprentices had to do. Such an unethical practice had to be stopped when the union highlighted the exploitation to the labour commissioner who ruled that such practices had to stop forthwith.

However, the workers, who were recruited, had to give an undertaking of good behaviour before they were allowed to enter inside the factory premises. The issue of productivity could not be resolved, as the norm set by the management was too stiff to meet by the workmen as demonstrated by the union's representatives.

MANAGEMENT-LABOUR RELATIONS

An epic battle ensues between the labour union(s) and the management of a company at the time of wage revision, normally once in three to four years. Every trick in the trade is adopted to outwit each other. Meanwhile discipline and production suffer during the pendency of the negotiations. It depends upon the culture of the company how it settles the demand put forth by the union(s). An enlightened management would accept most of the demands. However, it would also insist upon discipline and productivity improvement from the labour union(s)/employees over a period of time in return for meeting the wage increase and other benefits accruing to the employees. A long bitter controversy lasting months is good news for the company's competitors but not to the employees or to the management of the company in turmoil.

Case Study

A well-known large-scale company in Mumbai had employed a Personnel Manager (PM) who got on famously with the labour union leaders. It was an open secret that the PM was directing some of the actions of the labour union. During the labour-management negotiations, the union used to put up a list of about 100 demands. Most of these were at the direction of the PM. It was easy for the management to deal with such a pliable union. But people saw the ruse sooner than later and the labour union leaders who had became the henchmen of the management were kicked out of the labour union committee to be replaced by other leaders who stood their ground and wanted their just demands to be met. The new leadership shunned the PM and would have no truck with him. Unfortunately, the PM lost his clout with the management too and had to resign.

Moral: Such unethical practices don't help anyone in the long run. Management should have dignified, ethical and friendly relations with the labour union.

A management and a labour/employee union(s) are two sides of the same coin. There is traditional and historic bad vibes between the two and there is little trust between them. The employees/unions, rightly or wrongly, think the management creams off all the profits and they get a pittance in return. They cite the fabulous salary/perks/intangibles that accrue to the management officers while the employees have to beg for their share of the pie and get it only after a long bitter struggle. The concept of union leaders on the board of directors has not worked, except in rare cases. While a labour/employee union is desirable for collective bargaining, it should be responsible too. It should not do anything to 'kill the goose that lays the golden egg.' There are instances where the unions were able to extract the maximum advantage for their members from time to time but one fine day the company discovered that it had no money to pay even the wages and salaries of their employees. Fiscal discipline is an important task of a management and the employees/unions should appreciate the fact that all the profits cannot be divided among the employees. A company needs to have reserve funds for a rainy day.

As far as the disparity in the salary/perks of management officers and the blue/while collar employees, that would remain for ever and the moment that tends to become equal we could expect the talented people, the real brains behind the management, would find greener pastures elsewhere. That aspect should be kept in mind by everyone when parity in salary/perks is demanded for all employees irrespective of their talent, qualification and educational background. Parity in salary for one and all is nothing but a Utopian dream that comes true rarely, if at all. However, whether a new entrant should get a salary that is much higher than some of the experienced, and equally talented employees, should be considered seriously. The only way is to revise the salary/perks of employees regularly keeping in mind the market trends. However, that should depend upon the 'paying capacity' of the organization. That also applies to labour-management wage negotiations that are held once in three/four years. The demands should be reasonable and the company should be able to give such rises within its resources. Otherwise, such a company would enter the 'sick list' sooner or later.

It is stated, 'A management gets a labour union it deserves.' Maintaining the correct balanced relations is a tough task. However, there has to be a great degree of 'give-and-take' attitude and confrontation on every silly and trivial issue should be avoided for better relations. *The management and the labour/employees union should think not only of the present but also the future of the company and so should not indulge in any activity that harms the company's long-term business interests*. The only beneficiaries during a conflict in a company would be the competitors who would be delighted to grab that company's business too. Unionization is a ticklish issue, with its pros and cons. A few industries like the IT-related business do not encourage employees/labour unions to form within their business milieu. Collective bargaining cannot be abolished altogether as people have a right to form such unions/associations to safeguard their collective interests. In fact the managements too should not do anything to harm such unions but guide them, if needed, so that the relations between the union and management is based upon mutual trust and confidence.

11

Future of Management

—What the crystal ball tells

"What fuels long term business success?" is a question worrying the top business men who would like to unlock the secret that has been successfully adopted by long-standing successful corporations which continue to grow worldwide despite winds of change as well as stiff competition. The key is—newer methods of recruiting and retaining talent, allocating enough resources in key areas of business and formulating strategies for long-term growth. *The buzzword is Innovation*. To secure a lasting competitive edge, today's companies must reinvent management. Organizations need to provide a new route map for twenty-first century managers. Employees are smart enough to manage themselves provided they are given the tools in time and see that these are updated regularly. Moreover, a manager has to be a philosopher, friend, guide and coach to the employees and spend less time in chasing them or breathing down their neck. Trust begets trust and so the new era manager has to trust his/her employees more and more.

The role of a manager would be more and not less when facing the future with its numerous ramifications. The more knowledgeable he/she is the better. While a manager is expected to equip himself/herself with the latest gadgets, he might have to unlearn a few ones before starting on the new techniques. That is not easy but is needed in the dynamic world of business. However, a few techniques that have withstood time and age need not be given up. For example, "Customer focus" would always hold the first priority in any business.

The world is shrinking with national borders almost disappearing as far as trade, commerce and business are concerned. It is not much of an exaggeration to say the world is becoming a 'global village'. That is largely due to the reduction of tariff barriers thanks to the WTO (World Trade Organization) regime with less and less barriers for free trade and commerce. Such a move has spawned a variety of activities—acquisitions, mergers, take-overs and the like with foreign companies wanting to set-up their base in our country. Surprisingly, Indian businessmen too are becoming MNCs (Multi National Companies) by investing/acquiring foreign-based companies. Such a trend would continue in the coming years.

What is interesting to note is that business wants to spread global for which acquiring other companies is of paramount importance.

For instance, *Microsoft*, the world's biggest software company wants to spread its wings even further by acquiring the Internet Search Engine Giant, *Yahoo*, by offering an astronomical amount in billions of dollars. Whether such a move would succeed or not only future would tell.

We have our Indian origin but UK-based Lakshmi Mittal who has become the Steel King with a holding of steel companies in different countries of the world dominating steel production and distribution. Tata Companies have acquired Tetley branded tea in the UK. Kingfisher Airlines acquired Air Deccan, Jet Airlines took over Sahara Airlines and there are many examples where acquisitions and mergers have become commonplace to grow and consolidate one's position in the domestic as well as having a global presence. Such moves and counter moves would continue. Dynamics of companies spreading their wings with new strategies would be an important factor in the global trade and business.

The question that is being asked is, "What is the future of Management in such an ever changing world?" It would be naïve to believe it would remain just the same because we are comfortable with the *status quo*. Managers who thought their skills acquired during the college would suffice are feeling the heat when youngsters just out of college are becoming more technique savvy than themselves, often causing acute embarrassment. Education never stops and one has to keep abreast of the latest techniques that are making the corporate rounds. Whether every known management tool should be used is a matter of one's own judgment. *Choosing the right tool for the right application is a matter of common sense as well as one's own experience*. Managers are discovering that a tool that had worked well might not work equally well in a similar situation because of subtle differences in that particular situation. In other words, there is no substitute to one's own experience backed by sound judgment. That is an area where a senior experienced manager scores over a raw inexperienced but brilliant MBA fresh out of college and eager to show off his/her knowledge of tools and techniques. Surely, we would have more sophisticated and esoteric tools and techniques in the hands of managers and decision-makers of the future. Again, one's time-tested personal judgment backed by real time experience is no substitute to any tool.

With the world shrinking national borders, though still relevant, nations have begun to shed some of their restrictions, which earlier were thought to be unbreachable. That only means the manager of the future has to think global, yet with feet firmly on the ground locally. A problem that is likely to arise when dealing with cross-cultural employees is their attitude to work, general motivation and the subtle differences that could make or mar the efficiency of an organization. That is the reason the manager of the future has to be knowledgeable about the cultural differences of employees working for him/her. That could be within the country or outside as a senior manager could be handling several units spread out globally.

TECHNOLOGY AND INNOVATION

It is important to remember, "Dream is not that what you see while sleeping. . . . Dream is the thing which does not allow you to sleep." The onus is on the management to facilitate every employee to 'dream' that he/she could try to achieve something different, something novel.

> Every employee is an innovator given the right environment/incentive. That cannot be forced on any one but has to come from within.

Even a spark of genius at any particular moment is enough to kindle that imagination that could drive a person to create something unique that captures the imagination of the consumer. For instance, soluble coffee is a convenient way of consuming coffee, for its sheer ease of use at any time.

Technology has gone wild. Hundreds of new products/services are flooding the market every month. For instance, Personal Computer (P.C.)/Lap Top/Palm Top have become so common that practically every educated person owns one or has access to one. One wonders what the world would be without these innovations, which have revolutionized the way we operate in such a fast-paced, fast changing competitive world. Just imagine how the music world has changed. The bulky reel-to-reel tape recorder is now extinct replaced by a host of modern gadgets like the iPod that could store hundreds of music pieces and play when the user wants to play for his/her personal comfort through ear phones. CDs, audio/video are slowly but surely replacing audiocassettes for better quality of sound and for increased storage. VCRs, which were in vogue a few years ago are now almost extinct being replaced by high quality slim DVDs, which play better, lighter and cheaper too. There is a premium on innovation, with the R & D department getting sizeable funding by all companies as they realize that without timely R & D, no company could survive for long in the competitive world where innovation is the buzzword. However, a few companies opt to buy innovations/technology rather than start from scratch to catch up with competitors. Intellectual Property Right (IPR) is assuming greater importance in view of copyright act and threat of piracy and handiwork of copycats.

> "The largest emerging market in the world is green technology and India must exploit it."
>
> —*Al Gore, Nobel Prize Winner, Ex-Vice President U.S.A*

Innovators are few and far between, though sometimes a person could come up with some thing unique that captures the imagination of people. "Think, think, think. . ." is the mantra for getting that spark of innovation that could blossom into a product/service that is totally different from the existing range available in the market. For instance, model changes in the American car market is common, with changes every six months or so. The idea is to capture the imagination of the consumer that he/she should trade in the old model with the brand new one which has features that are different from the existing range of cars. However, often a mere cosmetic change is introduced without much of advantage to the user. It could be a different colour shade, small changes in the upholstery, a few additional features in the music system, GPS installation and so on. Consumers do consider exchanging their models, though there is no compulsion to do so.

> What is more important is that innovation should really benefit the consumer by way of savings in fuel consumption, additional features, enhanced comfort or safety.

MFI, multi-fuel injection system, is common these days as it gives better mileage. There are alternate fuels like gasohol, ethanol, and bio-diesel that claim to reduce exhaust gases of automobiles. Hybrid cars that run partly on petrol or diesel and partly electric batteries or LPG/CNG are coming out in the market as a result of emission restrictions and to improve fuel consumption. Hydrogen as fuel for cars is receiving attention. Gas-driven cars are in demand because these do not pollute the environment. Seat belts and airbags have become standard safety fixtures, which are absent in older models of cars. Surely, a few innovators have been able to conceive these add-on features and companies have invested in them for mass production. Such a trend to innovate products/services would continue in the future. Organizations have to be aware of timely innovations while senior managers should be part of such path-breaking teams. Often a leader of an innovating team draws attention to the possibility of an innovation in a particular field while his/her team could work on it and come up with concrete designs.

"You must innovate from tomorrow," would defeat the very process of innovation, as it is not something that comes every day at the press of a switch. Sometimes no ideas flash in the mind that could be of any use to the organization. Those who are in the R & D Department are under pressure to come out with new designs/process/products regularly. The management hopes with the investment in men and equipment the R & D would be profitable and productive soon. Such a hope sometimes is not realized as innovation is not time-bound, though organizations try to set targets, "We shall introduce newer products/services in the coming year." That is fine as a target but how do we ask the researchers to get something so novel out of thin air?

Here we should differentiate between basic research and R & D that often is a modification/improvement over an existing process/product/service. Basic research like innovation in nano-technology or discovering/inventing newer materials, or finding a cure for deadly diseases like AIDS/cancer is time consuming and no one could be sure when encouraging results would come out. *Extensive laboratory/field trials are needed before a certain drug could be approved by the governmental agency.* Companies are investing billions of dollars/rupees in basic R & D to get breakthroughs that could fire the imagination of consumers all over the world or find cures to deadly diseases.

On the other hand, development that involves modification/improvement in the existing product/process/service is not too tough as the developers could focus better on the final improvement that is marketable. For that to happen the researchers have to know the existing situation vis-à-vis competitors who could be already ahead in evolving better designs that could be turned into products that sell better as these have improved features, which fascinate consumers. For instance, a Flat screen/Plasma TV came out in the market as a few fastidious consumers were prepared to pay more for a TV that could improve viewing pleasure. More features such as Surround-Sound, Picture in Picture (PIP), more channels, and memory were built in to improve customers' satisfaction. Some of these have become standard features that have captured the imagination of viewers all over the world.

Ethics

> Ethical practices in organizations would receive higher priorities in future. That only means an organization should lay stress on the importance of transparency and openness at every level of the organization.

The top executives, the CEO and his/her team set the pace for ethical practices by declaring they would promote the highest level of ethics in business, come whatever may. For instance, if a junior executive cuts corners and bends rules due to exigencies of time or particular situation by avoiding tax that is due to the government, the entire organization is responsible for such a situation. "The buck stops here!" is what a CEO would state under such circumstances though the particular manager should be severely reprimanded and even dismissed for his/her unethical conduct that has brought a bad name for the organization. That is the reason the top executives would have to be 'walking and talking' examples of the highest form of ethics in all their dealings to avoid scandals like Satyam. *Best-managed companies go beyond mandated practices in corporate governance.*

Dealing with employees: An organization has people who are incidentally its employees. There are managements, which would like to get the best from every employee by paying the least so that they could show a healthy bottom line. That would be an unethical practice when the employees are cheated out of their deserving wages/salaries/perks/compensation just because the organization wants to make a profit at the cost of its own people. A few companies see to it that they are in the top half of the compensation package offered by companies in general in a specified region where they operate. However, only a handful would say, "We want to be the number one or two as far as pay packet and compensation are concerned." Some companies have the policy not to offer anything voluntarily to their employees. "Let them ask first. Then we shall consider and try to negotiate."

The clout of the labour unions is slowly but surely diminishing. For instance, IT industry does not encourage labour/employee unions to operate in their business milieu. Where labour/employee unions operate, it is generally once in a four to five year ritual to place demands by the unions and the management respectively. There is a dialogue followed by unrest before any 'demand' of the labour union is granted by the company management. That is the time for wage negotiations between the labour union(s) and management that drags on for months. A feeling persists that without a struggle the management accepts no demand. Moreover, the unions would tell their flock, "See, we fought so hard for your sake." Thus, there is a sense of achievement when something is extracted after a struggle.

Unfortunately, during the pendency of the demands of the union, there is unrest, violence, disruption of work and all sorts of pinpricks by both the employees, aided and abetted by the labour unions as well as management which wants to prove that 'might is right' by charge-sheeting unruly employees, especially those who are union committee members who instigate workers or they themselves cause harm to the management staff and its property. Go-slow is the norm during negotiations and indiscipline makes life miserable for everyone, especially the management staff which has to bear the brunt of the strong-arm methods of the employees, instigated by the union. In extreme instances, prolonged lockout results before normalcy is restored, with the demand by the management that the workers should give a 'good conduct' undertaking before they are allowed to enter the premises.

> The Management and the workers/employees and their labour/employee unions will have to realize that they are two sides of the same coin.

There is no progress unless both agree to work together and have a common goal to take the company to greater heights. The employees/unions often are right in assuming that the management is partial to their own management staff and the blue and white collar employees are given a step-motherly treatment. To some extent that is the truth because the managements have yet to adopt an enlightened policy that employees are assets treated the right way and they should be given their dues without too much struggle. *Best-managed companies are more employee-friendly, and focus on training and fair remuneration.*

Dealing with vendors: Without good and reliable vendors (also known as 'third parties') no company could hope to make everything it needs for its production/process/service which would be very uneconomical, even if someone attempts such a venture. Vendor relations will have to receive better attention. The tendency to 'milk the vendor dry' should give place to fruitful and productive partnership for mutual benefit and profit. In fact, in future the concept of 'vendor-on-the-team' would gain universal acceptance. However, a vendor who does not come up to expectation should be given all the technical/financial assistance necessary but if such help does not improve the vendor's quality, quantity or reliability, then there is no alternative but to drop such a vendor who could be a drag on the company rather than a help and a valuable partner. The CEO of a company should formulate the vendor policy, which should be fair and just and should be seen so by the vendors too. Interaction between the vendors and the parent company should be a regular feature for not only feedback but for improved relations that help in building and bonding long-term relationships. *Best-managed companies develop, monitor, and improve their vendors.*

Dealing with stakeholders: Stakeholders (shareholders) are the real owners of a business without whose support no organization exists. The stock market is an index of the worth of a share, subject to various factors internally as well as externally, which a stakeholder has invested. If the price goes up a stakeholder is happy if it goes down he/she thinks the company is doing badly and might even think of selling his/share when the opportunity arises. The only formal interaction between the stakeholders and the company management (represented by Chairman and Board of Directors) is during the Annual General Body Meeting (AGM), which is a big mela type of function where a few vocal shareholders voice their opinion about the organization and raise important questions or seek clarification. The management (Board of Directors) clarifies doubts of the shareholders and takes note of the suggestions.

> The shareholders, who are also the general public, want a company to continue to make profits, declare regular dividends and offer bonus shares when it could.

They would appreciate if 'freebies' were offered by the company—gift coupons, vouchers, free samples and the like. An "Open House" day(s) on the company premises would welcome shareholders to step in and get firsthand experience of their company. They could see what is being produced and how they are doing it. However, the shareholders would not tolerate unethical practices that bring a bad name to the company. They expect sound financial management, with proper audits at regular intervals, and they don't like a Satyam-type fiasco. A harmonious labour-management is what shareholders expect from the company they are part and parcel. *Indian companies are able to partner with their stakeholders to create value for society, while giving handsome returns to their stakeholders.*

Dealing with governmental agencies: Whether an organization accepts it or not, it is bound by a few governmental regulations which it has to comply. For instance the matter of labour laws, sales tax, excise duty, VAT and pollution control are some of the issues, which a company has to comply. We are still operating in some sort of permit raj that requires permit for setting up the company in a specified area/zone and for enhancing capacity level and so on. A few government officials like factory safety inspectors, and excise inspectors have the right of way to inspect any unit they wish. If the organization has to work within the limits set by the government rules, it has to do so without ifs and buts. No corners should be cut in meeting safety, labour regulations that includes fair wage and employment of child labour and pollution control limits laid by the government or its agencies. We will have to work within the system otherwise there would be chaos when there is a *lassier-faire* approach for setting up and running a business/industry/company. The issue of pollution has assumed greater importance as the public is concerned with the safety of the public by a factory which is producing toxic substances, People have not forgotten the December 3, 1984 Bhopal Gas tragedy that killed 3500 innocent people and injured 200,000 some of whom are still suffering the toxic effects of the deadly gas leakage from the Union Carbide Factory that produced toxic chemicals.

Dealing with NGOs/public/community: In the past an organization/company/corporation was not much concerned with the community milieu in which it was operating. The management philosophy was simple—make profit within the rules of the game prescribed by regulations. The concern for the community was either minimal or totally lacking. All these have changed to keep pace with the increasing concern by business for the society, community and the environment. Such concern would increase in the years to come, as companies want to be seen in a favourable light by the public.

> A business is not just a moneymaking device but also one that has to fulfil social, community and environmental obligations too.

A beginning was made when enlightened companies began to help the communities which were badly affected by natural disasters—droughts, earthquake, floods and tsunami. Not only money was donated to be spent in these natural disaster areas but also volunteers from the company went to the affected places to rescue people and take care of the sick and the injured.

Later on a few companies began to beautify gardens and parks nearby by adopting them for beautification with a commitment to maintain these for a specified period. Tree planting and environmental protection were the logical steps that followed indicating the commitment of the company to work to preserve the environment by means of financial and technical assistance, when needed. As a social commitment, some of them sponsored cultural events like music and dance to raise funds. Sports was another discipline where the companies did well to employ sportspersons to work for them but allowed enough time to spare so that they could train as well as take part in tournaments. Some companies made a policy to employ physically challenged persons as part of their community commitment.

Such commitments towards the society, community, and the environment would only increase in future, as organizations want to be seen as progressive by being part and parcel of the community and the nation they are working. A few organizations work closely with the NGOs in a few areas of activity by funding specific projects and sometimes render technical and administrative assistance too.

> "The NGO system, more influential than ever before, can empower people to find better localized solutions."
>
> —*Bill Clinton, 42nd President of USA*

Companies have ventured into the field of education too to fill the needs of the children of their own employees, which are also thrown open to the public. We could expect enhanced involvement of the companies in the coming years in various fields of interest to the general public. Organizations have to demonstrate visibly that they care for the society/community/environment in which they are operating. *Best-managed companies score high on corporate social responsibility.*

Environmental concerns are getting more and more serious with the activists spearheading movement against companies who pollute or degrade air, forest, land and water sources. Judicial activism is supporting environmental causes when it comes to setting up factories in eco-sensitive areas. The management of the future has to be abreast of the environmental regulations so that they take keen interest in being on the right side of the environmental laws in force from time to time. They have to take active part in Environmental Impact Assessment (EIA) before setting up a project in any designated area, which is a way of interacting with the public who are likely to be affected by the forthcoming project.

Special Economic Zone (SEZ): This is a concept to set up industries in some areas of a state. This has predictably run into rough weather as seen in Nandigram of West Bengal. Villagers who are affected by land acquisition are unhappy that they got a pittance of compensation. These SEZs could be turned into "Islands of Prosperity" once the local people are convinced that these are in their larger interest by providing better value for their land, improved job opportunities, and excellent infrastructure development. The various concerns of local people in the proposed SEZs should be addressed to sincerely, transparently keeping the people's interest in mind. SEZ is not such a bad idea as made out by some vested interests.

Empowerment

Managing with no/little control: From a rigid hierarchical structure, the classical 'top-down' organization, we have come a long way. That is because employees are getting to be smarter/better qualified/experienced than before. However, a few organizations still cling to the old and time-tested hierarchical organization, as they are not confident about any drastic change. The fact is some of the company managements do not trust the employees too much to give them more powers with a fear these could be misused or they would lose their importance if someone down the line starts taking important decisions without even consulting the higher ups.

Empowerment is the buzzword of present times.

> The more an employee is empowered the better, vouch senior managers who have empowered their people and found to their pleasant surprise that they not only accepted more responsibility but also started demanding more and more as people gained confidence.

Such an attitude is of great help as the seniors who could then concentrate on more vital aspects of management-career development, long-term strategy, budget, merger/acquisition, interfacing with the government/NGOs/public and so on. Such empowerment of employees is likely to be practised more and more in organizations that would also fulfil the aspirations of the employees who are eager to do more and be part of decision-making as well as long-term plans. Each and every person at each level of the organization desires to be empowered to help to build his/her career through multi-tasking and also for acquiring managerial skills that could help in dealing with problems at the workplace.

Training/Motivation

Practically every organization has some sort of induction programme for new employees which is to introduce the new employee to the organization he/she has joined. That could be a matter of a few days, or few weeks depending upon the employee's level. Some organizations rush through such induction process as they think that is a sheer waste of time and effort and should be completed somehow quickly. However, unless the new employee is exposed to the various aspects of the organization he/she might not be in a position to handle his/her assignment properly. Thus, the induction programme should not degenerate into a meaningless ritual but one that could prove useful to the employee and improve his/her effectiveness.

Training/retraining aspects would be given importance in the organization of the future in view of fast changing technologies, processes, methods and materials. Investment in such an exercise would payoff as the employee would acquire skills to help him/her do the job better. Every HRD has a cell to deal with induction/training/retraining. However, in view of the increasing complexities, the actual task of identifying sources for new training/retraining could be left to the department concerned. The HRD would negotiate with the sources that could provide such training. There are more consulting firms now, their number likely to increase in the coming years, which provide training of employees. It would be an advantage if some training programme modules were to be out-sourced to competent third parties after negotiation. Such an arrangement has advantages though they do have a few negative aspects too. That is because the consulting firm(s), unless it has studied the organization in depth, might not offer the kind of specific skills needed to help the employees to improve their skills. Hence it would be good to have a two-way communication with the consulting firm so that updating of the training module(s) could be done so as to tailor-made it for the particular needs of the organization.

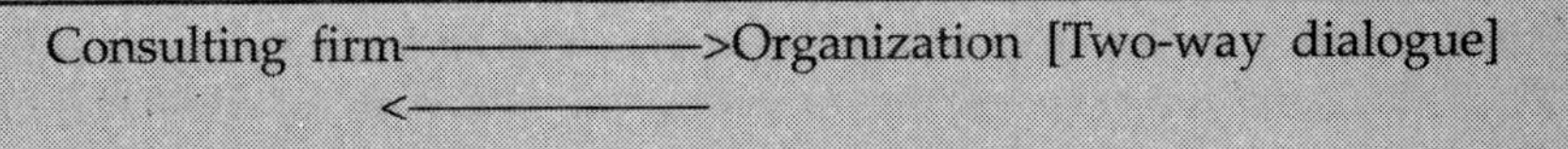

In-house training is an aspect that is catching on, with the induction of outside experts/consultants, as and when needed. A separate training facility, fully air-conditioned, amidst greenery in a quiet place, with fully equipped with computers, slide/projector, conference facility could be an asset to an organization that wants to take up in-house in a big way. However, the CEO and the senior managers have to be convinced that investment in in-house training is essential otherwise the programme could flounder after some time, with funds drying up. That is more so when there is a downturn in business. However, some organizations believe that is the ideal time to make in-house training an aspect of the organizational policy as they could concentrate on the training programme while the higher-ups are working out strategies to tackle the crisis situation. The faculty is generally taken from within the organizations, supplemented by outside experts/ consultants when the need arises. Such a training schedule should be structured and updated as a continuous exercise, covering each and every level of the organization that is likely to receive higher allocation of funds in the future to meet challenges due to technology and competition.

Motivation: Motivation is something inside a person that makes him/ her tick and give out the best without coercion. A number of incentives could help—monetary, recognition, promotion/career advancement, and foreign training/placement. An organization is constantly on the look out for actions to be taken to improve motivation of its employees as that is essential if the training/skills enhancement could be utilized better. A de-motivated employee is a drag on the organization and one bad apple could spoil the entire barrel. *That is the reason, every employee has to be motivated to work for the betterment of the organization that would also help the employee to derive benefits directly as well as indirectly.* There are experts/consultants in the field of motivation who are doing a yeoman service to the cause of improving motivation of people by their long and varied experience.

> But one aspect that should clearly be understood and appreciated is the fact that each person/organization is unique and so what has worked well in one might not work equally well in another organization. However, there are a few general guidelines.

For example, there is a need for tailor-made motivational packages in consultation with the organization concerned that could prove useful. Some of the motivational techniques—quality circle, group activity, suggestion box, zero defect, six sigma—have worked well in some organizations while others have fared a mixed bag of success. Such motivational programmes would increase in the future. The organizations have to do proper homework and assessment before deploying such methods/techniques in their organization. A few of them do something 'because others are doing it', that's like 'keeping up with the Joneses'. However, keeping employees motivated all the time is a matter of deep understanding of the psychology of the employees, which needs constant review after discussion with the employees. *A highly motivated workforce is an asset to an organization where the employees do not need to be told to improve their level of motivation to realize goals set by the management.*

Labour/management relations: Even during the best of times relation between the labour union/employees and the management is cool. There is no warmth in the relations due to several historical reasons. Some of the earlier strategies adopted by the management as well as union(s) are not conducive to a harmonious relationship between the two. In fact, ideally both of them should realize they are two-sides of the same coin and so have duties as well as responsibilities to each other for efficient working of the company/corporation/organization. We need more enlightened managements, employees and labour unions to tackle the various issues confronting a business instead of creating a division of 'we' and 'they'. The relations between the two should be based upon mutual trust and respect. *Confrontational approach of the past between management and labour/employee union(s) should be forgotten history if an organization has to survive in this competitive global market.*

In some sectors, especially the IT sector, unionization is not on but still the management has to safeguard the interests of its employees. Regular pay hikes/benefits should accrue to the employees though when there is recession, due to market fluctuations, such an automatic increase might not happen from year to year. In fact, when there is a downturn in the fortunes of an organization, employees might have to accept pay-cuts to tide over a difficult financial situation for the company. In other words, flexibility in salary/wages/benefits has to be accepted as part of any business due to cyclic variations. For instance the recent rupee appreciation is hitting the IT business's competitive edge when there is slow down in the US market that has effected several Indian IT companies as well as others in their export trade with that country. Such indicators have to be factored in future as far as possible by advance study of the likely trends and by taking timely actions in a pro-active manner. For instance, if the US economy has taken a recessionary trend, companies should explore markets of Asia, Europe and South America. To work out a specific strategy needs skills and consultations with experts in the field of finance, trade and commerce and economy especially the several International ramifications. The fact is the WTO regime has brought down trade barriers drastically, which trend would continue, with freer trade and commerce with nations than ever before. If we have to stay competitive then there is need to have expertise in the field of International laws, finance, trade and commerce.

Human side of the Enterprise

One thing is for sure—human relations within and without an organization/company/corporation/business is bound to receive unprecedented attention from top management as well as outside experts/consultants in future.

> Human capital is going to be a critical element in planning business and market strategies.

Managements have begun to give credit to their teams, which are made up of employees of several levels within the organization. If some employee is treated shabbily, the bad news spread. So also, for an out-of-the way goodwill gesture from a manager which has caused ripples of satisfaction all around. Employees desire that they be recognized as human beings with emotions and feelings and not by a salary/wage number. Even now a few managements think employees are 'liabilities' and would not think of putting them as assets. They think by paying wages/salaries/perks the contract between the employee and the management is over. "If an employee is unhappy that his/her problem. Why should we pander to that employee? We can always hire someone else," is the general feeling among managers brought the old fashioned way where boss-subordinate relation was dominant.

How do managers of the future treat their people under them? First of all, the employees should get the respect and consideration that is due to them and not as hired workers. *They would be given credit for the success of the team while the leader shares the blame too.* No one is made a scapegoat when something goes wrong.

The leader accepts responsibility for anything going wrong but does not pass on the buck to the team members. However, he/she would hold discussions with the team members to find out what went wrong, and not who went wrong, so that corrective measures could be initiated for the future.

Teamwork

A business success is due to total team effort. The leader no doubt leads from the front but without the active cooperation and contribution of each and every member of the team, success cannot be guaranteed. Teamwork should be preached and practiced by all the managers to build harmonious working teams that deliver. A good team spirit can do wonders especially when the chips are down. These are the occasions when the team members could help each other, talk to each other and find ways and means to get out of a difficult situation. A number of teams, formal or informal, could be working simultaneously in any one department. The coordination of such teams would be entrusted to one person, a senior manager. Managers of the future would be trained and motivated to create teams that pull together in the overall interest of the department/organization. *The more viable a team, the better for cohesiveness and improved team spirit*. There could be a few persons who are slow and uncooperative that might affect team working. How to bring such persons on board is a matter of deep concern as the team effectiveness could improve much more if these persons too are as good as others.

Leadership

The leader of the future is a person with farsighted vision

That person sparks the imagination of the people under him/her. Innovation is the key to success and so the leader has the onus of inspiring the team members to do something different and achieve greater success in their endeavours. A point that is going to be stressed more and more is that people should be trusted and there is no need to supervise them. *Thus the employees should be trained for multi-tasking so that they could perform a number of tasks that enriches one's own experience while increasing team's effectiveness too.*

The CEO of the future is a team leader par excellence. His/her aim is to make the company a brand name to reckon with in the business world. That person would set the company's benchmark against global best practices. Cross-cultural interface is getting more and more important as the units, after acquisition/merger/takeover, are spreading globally. That is a tough task and the CEO has to be culture-sensitive if that person has to carry the workforce with diverse backgrounds together in the effort to make the company world class.

Developing leadership quality in an employee is a formidable task.

A few bosses hesitate to go all out to develop a subordinate as a future leader. The reason is the boss feels threatened when a subordinate aspires to be a leader on his/her own. On the contrary there are enlightened managers who feel it is their duty to develop the people under them. In fact, they would be happy if some subordinate is good enough to replace him/her. The idea is that person who becomes 'redundant' in that position could then get another assignment and so the career development of employees could go on smoothly. That would be one of the major concerns of managers of the future who would strive hard to develop leadership qualities among their subordinates. However, it is quite possible only a few among the staff could have that leadership attributes that could be developed by training and exposure. We have a few leaders but many followers.

Organization

The trend is, as discussed in an earlier chapter, for the organization to develop horizontally with less number of layers of command. Moreover, there are innovative schemes like flexible hours, part-time work, home-based work, and on-line work to deploy a large number of capable persons, which would benefit the organization as well as the individuals concerned. Innovative ways to restructure an organization to meet the market/global trends that would benefit it is an on-going exercise. *Every organization has to be tailor-made to suit its needs, though a few time-tested broad guidelines help.*

The trend is to decentralize power as well as decision-making.

The idea is that heads of units spread geographically within a nation or across the globe know the local set-up, rules, procedures and employees better than a CEO sitting in a far away place trying to control the destiny of any particular unit. A close interface between the various units through regular contacts, such as tele-conferencing, phone calls, E-mails, and personal visits help to know a unit better than merely reading a report sheet every week. There is nothing like a telephone call to get details rather than read e-mail or get a FAX report. However, for orderly business, written reports are essential.

Made in India

Within a short time after liberalization and globalization, India has shown what it could offer to the world. It is now a welcome destination for many corporations for large investments as they find in abundance availability of trained and skilled personnel at competitive wages and salaries. BPO is a success story with many corporations setting up their call centers in our country due to competitiveness. Our software industry (IT) is a shining example what it could do given the opportunity to go global. Engineers and skilled persons who used to find overseas countries attractive for employment are realizing that India has much to offer with the additional advantages of culture and a friendly environment. "Made in India" label has made its mark worldwide. Some of our ancient monuments like the Ajanta and Ellora, Belur and Halebid, Khajuraho, Konark Sun Temple, Kutub Minar, and Taj Mahal have attracted thousands of tourists because they see in these monuments the work of the master craftsmen who fashioned these so lovingly and so skillfully. That was the creed of excellence nurtured through the years by master craftsmen.

Management as an art was perfected by our ancient rulers who ruled their people with wisdom and tender care. Justice was fair and rewards were many for efficient, honest and sincere persons. No doubt we have to follow the global trends in management with cross-cultural units to deal over the globe. *At the same time we should rediscover those nuggets of ancient wisdom, which worked so well in the past.* However, these have to be adapted to the present business milieu. Our Non-Resident Indians (NRIs) and persons with Indian origin have demonstrated that they are second to none with their outstanding work in various countries that they have adopted as their own, without forgetting their roots. *More research is needed to make our Indian management techniques better known in the world.*

> "Business must dream to transform some aspect of the world we have inherited." —*Mukesh Ambani*

A blind imitation of any management style has to give place to "Indian" management style that suits our culture. However, we should be open to any management idea(s) from anywhere that could prove beneficial to us in our own business milieu.

2008-09 was a gloomy year for the world economy with practically every country, including India, affected by global meltdown that resulted in acute financial crisis, job losses and lack of confidence in the ability of the rulers to set matters right. Banks and financial institutions have collapsed that have caused serious problems to investors. Governments intervened with huge bailouts to pay off bad debts and restore confidence in the global financial system. Millions of people have lost their jobs and the outlook in 2009 is not too rosy either. This only shows we need regulations to prevent such disastrous mismanagement by one and all. Fiscal prudence is the need of the hour. We have to create jobs by investing in infrastructure and give a boost to the economy by spurring consumer spending. It's doubtful if the economy would be the same as before given the enormity of the crisis. The CEOs and senior managers have their tasks cut out to manage a difficult and challenging situation with all their experience and skills using innovative but ethical means to stay afloat in a sea of crisis created due to various internal as well as external factors. Everyone has to stick to ethics of business strictly.

Bibliography

Books/Journals

Note : Here is a list of journals and books that could prove useful reading. This is neither complete nor comprehensive but given for guidance only. For information on a management book/magazine/journal, try to search through the Internet using Search Engines like *Hotmail, Google,* and *Yahoo*.

Journals

Academy of Management Journal
Business Standard
Business Standards
Business Today
Fortune
Harvard Business Review
HR Focus
International Journal of Applied Management and Technology
Journal of Business Technology
Management Issues
Managing Office Technology
Management Science
Management Today, U.K
MIT Sloan Management Review
Organizational Behaviour Management
Supervisory Management
Technovation
Wall Street Journal

Newspapers

Business Line
The Economic Times

Books

Ann, Gilley, *The Manager as Change Leader*, McMillan India Ltd., 2008 (Reprinted).

Brian, Tracy, *Hire and Keep the Best People*, Magna Publishing Co. Ltd., 2002.

Craig, E. Johnson, *Ethics in the Workplace*, Sage Publications, 2007.

Dourado Blackburn and Dr. Phil Blackburn, *Seven Secrets of Inspired Leaders*, Wiley-India, 2004.

Gary, Hamel, *The Future of Management*, Harvard Business School Press, 2007.

Hegde, Y.S. and Rajeshwari Krishna, *The A to Z of Management Skills*, UBSPD, 1993.

Howards, P. Greenweld, *Organizations*, Sage Books, 2007.

John, Adair, *Inspiring Leadership*, Viva Books, 2005 (Reprinted).

John, M. Huntsman, *Winners Never Cheat*, Wharton School Publishing, 2007.

John, P. Kotter, *Leading Change*, Harvard Business Press, 2007.

John, P. Kotter, *The Heart of Change*, Harvard Business Press, 2007.

John, Reh. F., *Your Guide to Management*, Harvard Business Press, 2007.

Linda, A. Hill, *Becoming a Manager*, Harvard Business Press, 2007.

Manu, Parashar, *8 Steps to Building Innovating Organizations*, Response Books, 2007.

Marcus, Buckingham, *Now Discover Your Strengths, How to Develop Your Talents and Those of the People You Manage*, Pocket Books, 2001.

Mark, Gerzon, *Leading Through Conflict*, Harvard Business Press, 2006.

Mary, Walton, *The Deming Management Method*, 1988.

Michael, J. Marquardt and Peter Loan, *The Manager as Mentor*, MacMillan India Ltd., 2008 (Reprinted).

Murthy, D.B.N., *Of Man and Management*, UBSPD, 1994, (subsequent reprints).

Nilakant, V., *Change Management*, Response Books, 2006.

Rajnish, Karki, *Competing With the Best, Strategic Management of Indian Companies in a Globalizing Arena*, Penguin Portfolio, 2008.

Rob, Goffee and Gareth Jones, *Why should anyone be led by you?* Harvard Business Press, 2007.

Roger, Martin, *The Opposable Mind*, Harvard Business Press, 2007.

Rustom, S. Davar, *Creative Leadership*, UBSPD, 1993.

Seema, Sanghi, *Towards Personal Excellence*, Response Books, 2007.

Shiomo, Maital and D.V.R. Seshadri, *Innovation Management*, Response Books, 2007.

Shombit, Sengupta, *Jalebi Management*, Response Books, 2007.

Spencer, Johnson and Kenneth H. Blanchard, *One-minute Manager.*

Sumantra, Ghosal, Gita Piramal, Christopher A. Bartlet, *Managing Radical Change*, Penguin Books, 2002.

Thomas, F. Cawsey and Gene Deszca, *Toolkit for Organizational Change*, Sage Publications, 2007.

Tom, Peters and Nancy Austin, *A Passion for Excellence*, Vintage Books, 1994.

Infuse, Inc, *Readings in Management,* Vol. 1, 1997.

The Tom Peters Seminar, *Crazy Times Call for Crazy Organizations,* Vintage Books, 1994.

———, *Corporate Responsibility,* Harvard Business Review, 2003.

———, *Hiring Smart for Competitive Advantage,* Harvard Business Press, 2007.

———, *Leading by Example,* Harvard Business Press, 2007.

———, *On Becoming a High Performance Manager,* Harvard Business Review, 2002.

———, *Managing Change,* Harvard Business Press, 2007.

———, *Manager's Toolkit,* Harvard Business Press, 2007.

———, *Managing Your Career,* Harvard Business Press, 2007.

Index

J

L

M

N

O

P

Q

R